W. H. (William Hurrell) Mallock

Atheism and the Value of Life, five Studies in Contemporary Literature

W. H. (William Hurrell) Mallock

Atheism and the Value of Life, five Studies in Contemporary Literature

ISBN/EAN: 9783743305830

Manufactured in Europe, USA, Canada, Australia, Japa

Cover: Foto ©ninafisch / pixelio.de

Manufactured and distributed by brebook publishing software (www.brebook.com)

W. H. (William Hurrell) Mallock

Atheism and the Value of Life, five Studies in Contemporary Literature

TOPICS OF THE DAY

LONDON : PRINTED BY
SPOTTISWOODE AND CO., NEW-STREET SQUARE
AND PARLIAMENT STREET

ATHEISM

AND

THE VALUE OF LIFE

Five Studies in Contemporary Literature

THE PROFESSOR IN THE PULPIT
TENNYSON UNDER THE SHADOW
GEORGE ELIOT ON THE HUMAN DESTINY
NATURAL RELIGION
ATHEISTIC METHODISM

BY

W. H. MALLOCK

AUTHOR OF 'IS LIFE WORTH LIVING?'

LONDON
RICHARD BENTLEY & SON, NEW BURLINGTON STREET
Publishers in Ordinary to Her Majesty the Queen
1884

All rights reserved

PREFACE.

THE FOLLOWING ESSAYS, though not originally published in connexion with each other, will be found to embody a consecutive train of thought, and to follow one another in a connected and logical order. They have been written at various dates during the past five years. The first four appeared in the 'Edinburgh Review,' and are now republished through the courtesy of Messrs. Longman. The last appeared in 'The Nineteenth Century,' and is republished in accordance with an arrangement made by myself with Mr. Knowles.

October, 1884.

CONTENTS.

	PAGE
PROFESSOR CLIFFORD'S LECTURES AND ESSAYS	1
TENNYSON'S BALLADS AND POEMS	83
GEORGE ELIOT ON THE HUMAN CHARACTER	147
NATURAL RELIGION	211
ATHEISTIC METHODISM, OR THE BEAUTY OF HOLINESS	307

PROFESSOR CLIFFORD'S LECTURES AND ESSAYS.[1]

THE volumes now before us are extremely welcome; and we shall begin our remarks on them by explaining why we say so. The late Professor Clifford was a very remarkable man, and he was remarkable for two reasons—first, for the genuine eminence that was due to his own genius; secondly, for the imputed eminence that was due to the admiration of his friends. For the first of these we entertain all respect, and we shall speak of it in respectful terms; but we do it no wrong if we say that it is altogether dwarfed by the second. Professor Clifford has grave claims on our attention, and not only does this view of him in no way detract from these, but in some ways it very largely increases them. If we study a man

[1] Lectures and Essays by the late William Kingdon Clifford, F.R.S. Edited by Leslie Stephen and Frederick Pollock, with an Introduction by F. Pollock. Two vols. 8vo. London: 1879.

because we think him really great, and desire to understand the exact quality of his greatness, we shall, without doubt, be doing a very important thing. But if we study a man mainly because he has been thought great by others, we may be doing a thing that is no less important, although in a somewhat different way. If the interest in the former case is more intense, in the latter it is more extended. A genius, as a genius, represents himself, and nothing more than himself. A man, as thought to be a genius, represents the judgments of those who have thought him one; and the less solid the ground that this opinion rests upon, the more significant does the opinion itself become. We cannot be sure, for instance, that a man is a judge of poetry because he takes pleasure in reading 'Hamlet;' but we can be sure he is not a judge of poetry if he takes pleasure in reading Martin Tupper. If we pass from poetry to philosophy, the matter is yet plainer. We may assent dutifully to profound truths without being ourselves profound; but we shall not emphatically endorse superficial falsehoods without being ourselves ignorant and superficial.

Let us now pass at once to Professor Clifford, and see the application of these remarks to him. His most obvious claim to notice was his great power as a specialist. He was a mathematician of a very high order, and, speaking merely of the outward events of his life, it was as a mathematician that his career was successful. But besides his mathematical powers he had a wide and accurate grasp of physical science generally; and he had a singular faculty, also, of imparting clearly whatever he knew clearly. In this way he became, very early in life, a powerful and prominent figure in the world of scientific thinkers; nor, as we read his lectures, and reflect upon his personal character, can we at all wonder at the high position he occupied. But this position could by no means content him; he could not but look further. The scientific world, as compared with the world in general, was really, he saw, only a limited *coterie*, limited not only in point of numbers, but in point of the questions with which it was supposed to busy itself. How absorbing and vast these questions were no man knew better than Clifford, but he knew also that there was another question beyond

them, to which they were all subordinate.
This, in his own language, was the question of
'right and wrong;' or, in other words, the
question of how to live and what ends to live
for. This was the only enquiry, he said, that
concerned all of us; and it was further the
supreme concern of each. Man is born to act,
not to think and to know. Know and think he
must, and he must know and think accurately;
but this as a means only, not as an end. 'Our
interest,' Clifford said, in speaking of the physical sciences, 'lies with so much of the past as
may serve to guide our actions in the present,
and to intensify our pious allegiance to the
fathers who have gone before us and the
brethren who are with us; and our interest lies
with so much of the future as we may hope will
be appreciably affected by our good actions now.
Beyond that, as it seems to me, we do not know,
and we ought not to care.' It was his ambition,
therefore, to emerge from the domain of special-
ists, and to become a power in the domain of
practical life. He was not content with being
an instructor of students; he proposed also to
be a leader of men. Nor was his ambition here
of at all a limited nature. He saw the disorder

of the world, its painful perplexities of thought, and its chaos of conflicting motives, and he sought in the midst of this to inaugurate a new order, and by entirely new means. His schemes were co-extensive with the whole of human life. There was no force of passion or of faith, of self-approval or contrition, of joy or pain, with which he did not consider himself well qualified to deal. This assertion may at first sight appear startling; and doubtless, made bluntly, it would have startled Clifford himself. But we shall see very shortly that it is neither more nor less than the truth.

It must not be supposed, however, that Clifford's practical schemes and teachings at all superseded his more special studies. The former, as he conceived them, were but the fulfilment of the latter, and it was mainly the latter, he thought, that made him fit for the former. He did not say that scientific knowledge was inferior to practical knowledge, but that practical knowledge must be made scientific. 'What,' he asked, 'is the domain of science? It is all possible human knowledge which can rightly be used to guide human conduct.' And when knowledge, with a view to such guidance, had been enlarged and sifted by scientific methods, a complete revolution, he conceived, would take place in the whole of it. In this revolution, as we have said already, he aspired to play a prominent part. What was the part he actually did play in it is what we propose to enquire in the present article. Of his merits as a professor we shall say but little. We shall confine ourselves to considering how far those merits had fitted him to be an instructor of the world in general.

Now, our own verdict is that they had not fitted him at all; nor should we consider him in this capacity as worth discussion if it were not for one reason. That reason is the reverence that has been given him in England by those of his own way of thinking; and these are none other than that school of science and of progress which at the present moment has secured the ear of the world. If, therefore, in Clifford's writings we find but little of the sort of wisdom we are speaking of, we shall find what has passed for wisdom with those who pass for wise; so much so that in the volumes now before us we seem to have a reflection of the state of philosophical knowledge and practical sagacity amongst those who conceive themselves now to be the high-priests of humanity and the directors of human destiny. Similar reflections may, of course, be found elsewhere; but we doubt if we can find any so complete, and we may add so flattering, as here. Clifford was in every way fitted to be a representative man, in virtue alike of his strength and weakness, his breadth and narrowness, and also of his character, his education, and the general tenor of his life.

It is to this last subject that we now propose to proceed, as, in considering his general teaching, it will throw much light on the matter. It is his own observation that one of the chief steps in psychology was 'Hartley's idea of *mental chemistry*.' We are ourselves about to act on an idea somewhat similar, and apply to Clifford's life what we may call biographical chemistry. We will explain our meaning further. The practical teachings of Clifford, like those of his school in general, have been given to the world as the first fruits of a new era, and they are supposed to be based on reformed methods of study. We, on the contrary, conceive their origin to be entirely different. We conceive them to have nothing to do with reformed methods, or to be at best connected with them in a very secondary way. We believe them to belong almost exclusively to the old order of things, and that the true explanation of them is to be found not in the matured theories of their advocates, but in their early education, the circumstances of their lives, and the moral atmosphere they breathed while their characters were in the process of formation. We believe, in other words, that these teachings represent not the voice of science, but the voice of a certain section of society, remarkable in practical matters for amiability, simplicity, and prejudice, and, above all, for religious feeling. Nothing, we think, would show this more clearly than the examination we are about to make of the life of Professor Clifford. This, for our present purpose, need be only a very simple one, and Mr. Pollock's brief memoir will supply us with nearly all the materials that are requisite.

William Kingdon Clifford was born in 1845 at Exeter, where his father for a time was one of the chief booksellers, and afterwards, on retiring from business, a respected and active magistrate. The first fifteen years of his life

Clifford passed in his native city, and received
the best education that its schools could offer
him. Towards the end of this period he showed
marked signs of ability. He distinguished
himself in the University Local Examinations,
and in 1860 he went to King's College,
London. It was here that, for the first time,
his special powers developed themselves, and
he was recognised as a mathematical genius
of peculiar promise. He remained at King's
College for three years. Towards the end of
that period he went up to Cambridge, and
gained a minor scholarship at Trinity College,
and in 1863, at the age of eighteen, he began his
life there. Here he gained a reputation of a
somewhat varied kind, not only as a thinker
and a student, but also as a successful gymnast; and his biographer tells us of him that,
of all public testimonies to his merits at Cambridge, a paragraph in 'Bell's Life' was the one
that pleased him best. The regular course of
reading that is marked out for undergraduates
seemed to him at once narrow and narrowing,
and, though anxious for a good degree, he could
not resist endangering his best prospects by
straying in search of knowledge far beyond the

appointed boundaries. In this way, from an academical point of view, much of his time was completely wasted; and yet such were his talents and so great his powers of work, that at the end of his fourth year he came out Second Wrangler, and was also second Smith's prizeman. In the next year, when he was but twenty-three, he was elected a fellow of his college. Two years later he took part in the English Eclipse expedition, and saw something of foreign travel, both in its pleasures and its hardships. Another year passed, and he was elected Professor of Applied Mathematics at University College, London. He was now only twenty-six, and in another three years, when he was still short of thirty, he was elected Fellow of the Royal Society. In the following year he married, and, so far as we can presume to judge, all life seemed to be growing bright for him. But the promises of the future were too soon to be blighted. His assiduous work, in which he never spared himself, had been too much for even strength like his, and he had hardly been married a year before signs of pulmonary disease were observed in him. So grave did these appear that he was obliged, though with extreme reluctance, to accept a six months' holiday, which he spent in Algiers and in the south of Spain. This rest, for the time, was of great benefit to him. He returned to England much recruited, and, though still considered by the doctors extremely delicate, he continued for a year and a half longer a life of intellectual labour. By-and-by, however, a relapse came. He was working hard at the time, and he still refused to spare himself. At the same juncture his father died, and the shock of this loss was a fresh and severe strain. Every circumstance seemed to combine against him, and his own restless mind, which was more than ever occupied with work, was his worst enemy. His weakened system could bear up no longer, and his doctors now warned him that he was in a state of imminent danger, and that he must at once leave England. In the April of 1878 he and his wife started for the Mediterranean. Four months of travel again brought their benefit, and the invalid returned in August seemingly much better. The improvement, however, did not last long. In a few weeks he again overtried himself, a relapse took place, and 'from that day,' says his biographer, ' the fight was a losing one.' All that could be done for him his friends did, and through their solicitous counsels, and, we believe, attended by some of them, he again tried what a milder climate could do for him, and sailed for Madeira at the beginning of 1879. But it was all in vain. He gained nothing more than a two months' reprieve, and on March 3 of that year he died.

Such is the rough sketch of Clifford's life in its main outer incidents. His inward history we shall consider presently, but there is a certain tribute due to him which we shall first pause to pay. If we think of Clifford himself as a private character, the principal task before us is a singularly ungrateful one. It is a task that will consist of entirely adverse criticism. Clifford, as in a few moments we shall have to look at him, will be not a private character, but a public teacher, and we shall see him in this capacity as one of the bitterest and most unflinching opponents of everything that in general the world calls religion—a contemptuous and obtrusive denier of God, of soul, and of immortality. And we shall further see him as replacing the denied doctrines by others which, tried by his own canons, we shall show to be entirely baseless. But just as his merits as a man must not blind us to his faults as a teacher, so his faults as a teacher must not blind us to his merits as a man. The two in his case seem eminently separable, and we desire as distinctly as we can to separate them. Nor must anything we shall say presently about the former be held to indicate that we doubt or forget the latter. Of a man's intellectual eminence there is perhaps no worse judge than an admiring and affectionate friend. To a man's personal excellence there can be no better witness. And as to Clifford's private character, it seems that all his friends were agreed. Rarely, we fear, can it fall to the lot of anyone to inspire an intimate circle with such a deep and tender regard as Clifford did. Clifford's own circle, indeed, as his biographer tells us, was composed for the most part of what we may call kindred spirits, and his extreme opinions, which he never disguised from anyone, could be no offence to them, as to outsiders they could not fail to be. But even such outsiders were partly disarmed of their anger by his truthfulness and his severe simplicity. Mr. F.

Pollock's memoir is not perhaps remarkable as a piece of biographical art; but the affection he expresses for his friend is a fact of real significance, and the details of that friend's character, which he gives us with a touching tenderness, we may receive with implicit confidence—a confidence all the greater because the language used is so moderate, and no attempt is made to disguise certain slight imperfections. Thus both in manner and dress we gather that Clifford was generally uncouth and careless, and his laughter especially knew no conventional restraints. His humour, too, would seem to have been somewhat cumbrous, though much admired by the society in which he lived. Such defects as these, however, are only trifles, and by many of his friends they were probably thought merits. What we wish here to dwell upon are his deeper and rarer qualities. As a friend he was genial and unselfish, and, above all, constant and genuine. Even his enmities and disapprovals were softened by a natural charity, and, if he met his worst foe suddenly, his first impulse would have been to shake hands with him. As a companion he had many endearing qualities. In his eagerness in his own pursuits there was something catching. He forced his friends to share it, as if by some happy magic, whilst he was equally ready himself to feel with them in turn. 'But the real expression,' says Mr. Pollock, 'of Clifford's varied and fascinating qualities was in his whole daily life and conversation, perceived and felt at every moment in his words and looks, and for that very reason impossible to describe.' If we may be allowed to cite a valuable private testimony in corroboration of this remark, we may add that so keen an observer as Lord Houghton has, in our hearing, spoken of Clifford in almost exactly the same words; and after two such witnesses we need seek for no other. Truthful, affectionate, laborious, self-denying, and devoted, the moral life of this professional atheist may indeed put to shame not a few professional Christians. Mr. Pollock says further that it is a 'rebuke' to the defenders of Christianity. This, however, is a very different statement, and, as we shall see presently, an altogether untrue one.

Let us now return to what is of more direct concern to us. Let us return to Clifford as a teacher on practical matters—as a typical spokesman of our modern ethical atheism—and see what was his inward history, and how his opinions formed themselves. He was, as we have seen already, born in a cathedral town, and the first fifteen years of his life were passed almost under the shadow of the cathedral towers. Nor was this an outward fact only; it corresponded in his case, as we shall see was natural, to an inward one. Those were the palmy days of the Anglican or High Church party. It was then a real power in the English world of thought; much of the intellect of the country was attached to it; and at Exeter especially, under the celebrated Henry Phillpotts, its influence over many minds could hardly fail to be prevalent. In Clifford's case this influence seems to have been heightened by every circumstance. His father, in his business capacity, dealt largely in devotional books and bibles; and his high character and his superior position thus specially connected him with the ecclesiastical body. He was, indeed, pre-eminently a churchman's bookseller. At the back of his shop, under a glass case, stood a model of the west front of the cathedral, exquisitely carved in rush pith, the work of one of his own family, and regarded with a double reverence, both for the skill displayed by the artist and the character of the edifice represented. Such were the circumstances that surrounded young Clifford during the first fifteen years of his life—years in which the mind is open to all impressions, and which determine, more than any others, the feelings, if not the thoughts, of a man. And of Clifford it would have been said by a High Churchman that these early years did their best for him. His natural character was, it seems, deeply religious, and he grew up a devout and earnest Anglican. Nor did the faith of his boyhood desert him when he went to London, and must have been brought into contact with other ways of thinking; nor did it fail him even during his undergraduate course at Cambridge. Despite all the new knowledge that his scientific studies brought him, he still believed his Bible; he still revered his prayer-book; and a crucifix, as we have been told by one who knew him, hung on his bedroom wall, when he was first a fellow of his college. But about this time, as we gather from Mr. Pollock, an inward change was beginning in him, and the theology to which he had hitherto trusted began to seem vulnerable to his maturing powers of criticism. His religious faith, however, was as yet in no way weakened, only his belief in a certain Christian position. All truth must, he believed, be in harmony, and science and history he believed to be a part of truth; but he was growing convinced that science and history were not in harmony with the Anglican theory, and all his problem now was to find a religious system with which they should be. The direction his thoughts took will surprise many. They turned, not, as might seem natural, to the rationalising or the Broad Church School, but to the Church of Rome itself. Nor was this, in Clifford's case, any idle dallying. He set himself to study the Catholic theologians; he acquired some real knowledge of St. Thomas Aquinas, and used all his ingenuity and his scientific acquirements in defending the Catholic position. In his views at this time there was nothing of the spirit of compromise. He maintained to the fullest the authority of religious dogmas, and he held that they should be received implicitly without demand for proof. Such truths, he believed, were beyond scientific proof, and were only apprehended by man through 'a special theological faculty, or insight.' 'And he actually,' says Mr. Pollock, 'defined superstition as "a belief held on religious or theological grounds, but capable of scientific proof or disproof."'

'When or how,' says Mr. Pollock, 'Clifford first came to a clear perception that this position of quasi-scientific Catholicism was untenable, I do not exactly know.' We may ourselves remark, however, that it could not have lasted for more than two years after his having gained his fellowship. 'But I know,' Mr. Pollock adds, 'that the discovery cost him an intellectual and moral struggle, of which traces may be found here and there in his essays.' According to the same authority, this profound change of view was accomplished gradually, and 'without any violent reaction, or rushing to the opposite extreme.' On such matters Mr. Pollock has a right to speak with confidence, but we have reason to think that he is here perhaps mistaken. A story is told of Clifford, by one who knew him at this time, which would lead us, on this matter, to an exactly opposite conclusion. Clifford, as we have said already, had been wont to keep a crucifix in his bedroom, we believe for devotional purposes. One morning this revered symbol was found inverted, and placed upon it was a Phrygian cap of liberty. For the truth of this story we cannot ourselves vouch, but the source it came from seemed to us to be trustworthy; in itself it does not look like an invention, and it is also in harmony with many subsequent facts which Mr. Pollock himself tells us, and which Clifford's own words bear witness to. But, however sudden may have been his final break with Christianity, the beliefs with which he sought to replace the loss took some years in settling themselves; and, in spite of whatever Mr. Pollock may say, Mr. Pollock's own statements show that there was at first something 'extreme' in them, which Clifford afterwards modified. Thus he was inclined at first to think that he found in the doctrine of evolution something that far more than made up for what he lost in theology. He rushed from the sorrow of loss into the joy of discovery 'For two or three years,' says Mr. Pollock, ' the knot of Cambridge friends, of whom Clifford was the leading spirit, were carried away by a wave of Darwinian enthusiasm: we seemed to ride triumphant on an ocean of new life and boundless possibilities.' Like most other young men in the same stage of development, Clifford turned his thoughts towards the politics of republicanism. He conceived an enthusiastic admiration for Mazzini; he read and quoted the poetry of Mr. Swinburne, and thought 'Songs before Sunrise' some of the wisest and most precious poems ever written. All this was bound up closely with his scientific theories; and Mazzini he regarded as the priest, and Mr. Swinburne as the prophet, of evolution. He seems indeed, at this time, to have worked himself into a feverish and artificial state of excitement about the prospects held out to him by his new view of things. 'Shall there not,' he wrote in a notebook during his later days at Cambridge, ' be a new revelation of a great and more perfect cosmos, a universe fresh-born, a new heaven, and a new earth? *Mors janua vitæ;* by death to this world we enter upon a new life in the next. . . . The new incarnation may need a second passion, but evermore beyond it is the Easter glory.' The main definite idea that was embodied in this excitement was 'a conception,' as Mr. Pollock puts it, 'of freedom as the one aim and ideal of man. . . . It included Republicanism as opposed to the compulsory aspect of government and traditional authority in general, but was otherwise not bound to any particular

theory in politics. Indeed it forbade binding oneself irrevocably to any theory whatever; and the one commandment of freedom was thus expressed: " Thou shalt live and not formulise."
 . . . "There is one thing in the world," Clifford wrote at this time, "more wicked than the desire to command, and that is the will to obey."'

But this stage of thought was only a passing one. When he quitted Cambridge, at the age of twenty-five, and removed to London as a professor at University College, his views upon such subjects began slowly to be changed and modified and he was probably aware himself that they were not yet determined, since for five years longer he never gave them publicly any direct utterance, or began his ministry of practical teaching and prophecy. During these five years indeed, he published but six essays, and the subjects of them were remote from common life, although in reality, closely connected with it. In the February of 1870 he delivered a discourse before the Royal Institution on 'Theories of the Physical Forces,' which was printed in the 'Proceedings' of that body. He delivered a lecture at Manchester two years afterwards on 'Atoms,' and six months later in the same year, another lecture before the British Association, at Brighton, on the 'Aims and Instruments of Scientific Thought.' In March, 1873, he again lectured before the Royal Institution, his subject this time being 'The Philosophy of the Pure Sciences;' and in 1874 he lectured on the 'Beginning and the Ending of the Earth,' and on the 'Connexion of Mind and Body.' In these discourses, as their several titles denote, what he mainly aimed at explaining (and he did this with a most admirable lucidity) was the chief conclusions that modern science had come to concerning the constitution of matter, the history of the material universe, the connexion of the brain with consciousness; and further, though in a less successful and more faltering way, the nature of scientific knowledge as a whole, regarded from the metaphysical stand-point. But he touched only here and there, far off and indirectly, on such questions as morals and religion, and the practical hopes of the human race. Signs, however, are not wanting that it was to these questions he was gradually leading up, and that it was on these that he was preparing himself to speak before long with authority.

It was during this period, as his biographer

tells us, that his philosophy, as distinct from his science, took its final shape, and the lectures themselves show us how continually his mind was dwelling on it. We find him not only dealing with atoms, with heat, with the structure of the nervous system, but with object and subject, the Me and the Not-me, the existence of necessary truths, and the uniformity of nature in the case of conscious action. More than this too, we find that he has been busy with history, and that he has been endeavouring diligently to discover in it his philosophy teaching by example. Everywhere there is a sound of active mental preparation, and we feel that the forces are being massed for some more practical purpose. He is placing and pointing his artillery, that he may command human life. He defines progress for us, and tells us it is the same thing as science. He gives the general history of 'light and right' during the past two thousand years; how these existed for eight centuries on the shores of the Mediterranean, till, under the blighting influence of the Church, they 'went into abeyance,' and there ceased to be such a thing as 'goodness' in Europe—or would have ceased, had it not been for Arab or for Jew, who saved the sacred treasure from the rage and hatred of Christianity, which was nothing, in Clifford's judgment, but a power of 'disease and delirium.' Human history, he tells us, is the history of the progress of man; 'the progress of man is one with scientific thought;' for nearly 'twenty-two centuries,' he adds, the upward life of humanity has depended on one sacred book for its chief 'guide and encouragement,' and this is not, as is commonly supposed, the Bible, but the Propositions of Euclid. The meaning of all this we shall see presently. As yet he had not expressed it plainly. But he comes nearer to practical questions in other places. In 'Body and Mind' we see that the questions of 'fate and free-will,' of immortality, and of responsibility, are pressing close upon him; and in 'The First and Last Catastrophe,' in which he deals with the age and the duration of the earth, he does actually utter his first words of preaching. Towards the end of this lecture he says that the greatest of all our interests is bound up with the 'consciousness that exists upon the earth,' and that corresponds part for part, with the brain of the organised being. For all organised beings on the earth, some day or other, there is in store a final destruction, and for those who can see the force of scientific evidence the conclusion seems inevitable that all human consciousness will be finally destroyed with them; and 'it is a very serious thing,' says Clifford, 'to consider that not only the earth itself and all that beautiful face of nature we see, but also the living things upon it, and all the consciousness of men and the ideas of society which have grown up upon the surface, must come to an end. We who hold that belief must just face the fact and make the best of it. . . . Do I seem to say, "Let us eat and drink, for to-morrow we die?" Far from it. On the contrary, I say "Let us take hands and help, for this day we are alive together."'

The year in which these words were written may be said to have closed Clifford's period of mental preparation. The year following, he made his first appearance as a professed authority on the most momentous and profound of questions; and he began his utterances with no uncertain sound. A book had appeared about this time, called 'The Unseen Universe,' the work of two eminent men of science, who sought by certain ingenious theories to reconcile modern materialism with Christian theology, and especially to find a place in it for the belief in our personal immortality. The publication of this work loosened Clifford's tongue, and set free the thoughts and feelings that had been so long gathering. And what seems to have excited him in it was not the method of the authors, but their aims—the special doctrines which they were desirous of defending. Since the days, five years back, when Clifford was studying Aquinas, a change had indeed come over him. Then, if he must lose religion, the loss would, he felt, be a heavy one. Even fifteen months ago there seemed to him a profound sadness in it. But now his mood was different. What we saw him once regretting, we now find him hating. He can hardly speak of a Christian doctrine except in the language of parody; he seems nervously anxious to be as offensive as possible, and his voice seems to vacillate between a sneer and a forced giggle. Towards the end the note changes somewhat, and the young professor of thirty concludes with this awful warning :—

'Only for another half-century let us keep our heavens and "hells and gods." It is a piteous plea; and it has soiled the hearts of these prophets, great ones and blessed, giving light to their generation, and dear in particular to our own mind and heart. These sickly dreams of hysterical women and half-starved men, what have they to do with the strength of the wide-eyed hero, who fears no foe with pen or club? . . . That which you keep in your heart, my brothers, is the slender remnant of a system which has made its red mark on history, and still lives to threaten mankind. The grotesque forms of its intellectual belief have survived the discredit of its moral teaching. Of this what the kings could bear with the nations have cut down; and what the nations left the right heart of man by man revolts against day by day. You have stretched out your hands to save the dregs of the sifted sediment of a residuum. Take heed lest you have given soil and shelter to that awful plague which has destroyed two civilisations and but barely failed to slay such promise of good as is now struggling to live among men.'

Having thus traced Clifford's opinions up to the time when they took their final consistency, we will now examine in detail what his formed system was. Ultimately and essentially it was a practical, an ethical system; but the ethical part of it rested on three others, which we may call, with sufficient accuracy, the physical, the metaphysical, and the historical; and these, as treated by him, we will now consider separately. Numerous and diverse as are the details of all three, for Clifford their primary outcome was one very simple message—there is no God, no soul, no future life. We say this is what he learned from them primarily; because in a secondary way he looked to science doubtless for many conquests over nature that would ameliorate man's condition, and to history for many lessons that would guide his conduct, in addition to that general system by which religion was to be superseded. But to destroy religion—that soiling power, that grotesque threatener of mankind, that awful plague, that portentous phantom, the offspring of disease and hysteria—to destroy this, and to leave the ground clear for what was better, seems to have been the first personal anxiety of Clifford with regard to his own inner convictions, as well as the first practical step in the general reconstruction of thought. That Clifford's conversion to unbelief was genuine it is not possible to doubt. He yielded with sorrow and reluctance to what he thought overwhelming evidence. But he seems subsequently to have been conscious that the peace bought by the victory was not proportionate to the pain he had endured in gaining it. A vague misgiving seems still to have haunted him, that the religion he had rejected might, after all, be the true one, and that the sufferings he had undergone might be sufferings in the cause of falsehood. That he respected these misgivings, or seriously entertained them, we do not for a moment mean. We mean the exact contrary. He resolved not to entertain them; he resolved to despise them. He regarded them as the voices of an intellectual tempter whom it was his business to exorcise; but still they were there with their disturbing whisper, continually forcing him to exclaim, 'Get thee behind me, Satan!' There is reason to believe that this was the case from the evidence of certain of those who knew Clifford. But, even were evidence of this kind wanting, the same fact might, we think, be gathered from his writings. In physics, in metaphysics, and in history, underlying all his other interests, there seems to have been a nervous, half-unconscious, and almost instinctive watchfulness over every alleged fact and every theory, to see whether, directly or indirectly, it would give the least assistance to theology; and if it would do this, Clifford was prepared to reject it. It is this, we think, that accounts for the bitterness that is so often traceable in his writings. He is still afraid that he may have scotched the snake, not killed it; and he is perpetually stamping on it, to make sure that it shall not revive.

This is least manifest in his dealing with physical questions, but even here it is distinguishable. Of his physical creed we need not speak at length, because he had himself little to do with elaborating it, and its outlines are also familiar to the world at large. Clifford was not, nor did he profess to be, a specialist in any department of physical knowledge. But he was a diligent and accurate student of all the best authorities, and he could often explain experiments and discoveries more clearly than could the discoverers and experimentalists themselves. But though, in his knowledge of the detailed facts of physics, he was thus far removed from the lay world in general, the most momentous lessons that those facts seemed to teach him were only those that the lay world could appreciate; and these, though, as we have said, familiar now to most of us, it will be well to state briefly. In the first place, then, all nature is uniform. There has never been in it anywhere any breach of continuity; and it follows from this—the following are Clifford's own words—'that the state at this moment of any detached fragment [of the universe], say a particle of matter at the tip of my tongue, is an infallible record of the eternal past, an infallible prediction of the eternal future. . . . As the history of eternity,' he adds, 'is written in every second of time, so is the history of the universe written in every point of space.' Its history as a whole, our own limited powers have not permitted us to discover. It is, however, self-existent. It has been the work of no conscious intelligence; and, so far as we know, *design* is altogether peculiar to the animals living upon the earth. Consciousness cannot exist without a brain; and the only rational conception of an intelligent Deity would oblige us to suppose the whole universe to be a brain. But in this case, Clifford argues, God could know nothing of human actions, and he could only influence the course of events by his weight. Any such notion as this, however, we may set aside.' ' The universe,' he says, ' is made up of atoms and ether. There is no room in it for ghosts.' But though certain facts about the constitution of matter generally are all we can arrive at when dealing with the remoter distances of time and space, with regard to our own system, and especially our own planet, we can speak with more confidence. It is this last that most nearly concerns us; and 'what we know with great probability,' Clifford says, is this. Between one and two hundred millions of years ago, the earth was a liquid in a state of intense heat, but in a constant process of cooling. About the date just indicated 'there was,' he says, 'a catastrophe, which induced a new rate of cooling;' and we 'come to a time when the earth began to assume its present state.' The immense distance of that time from our own it is hard for us to realise; but we may gain some better notion of it if we represent as six years, the six thousand years for which it is commonly said that man has possessed a history, and then say that the time we are speaking of was about five hundred years ago. If Adam had been born a year or two before the death of Lord Beaconsfield the present earth would have been born about the time of the battle of Agincourt. At that date there would have been upon its surface no life, no soul, no consciousness—neither thought, nor emotion, virtue, or humanity. But Clifford agrees with Dr. Tyndall in saying that there would have been 'the promise and the potency' of them all. Whatever it may be that we commonly call matter, all that we call

D

spirit was then potentially contained in it; and about the date just indicated the first beginnings took place of what now is human life—took place by spontaneous generation. We may refuse to believe this, and say that life came from elsewhere. But whenever Clifford contemplated this only possible alternative, 'an invariable monitor,' he said, 'of which I can give no rational account, invariably whispers "Fiddlesticks!"' His beliefs from this point were the beliefs now so widely current. By some process or processes of evolution, amongst which the survival of the fittest was an important, though not the only element, life grew more and more complex, more and more organic, more and more conscious, until at last, from some non-human parents, the first human beings appeared on the earth's surface. A high scientific authority in Germany maintained that this last and central doctrine was not yet proved, and that we had no right to teach it, as yet, as true. This seems to have exercised Clifford's mind considerably, and his last literary work was an answer to it, which is for many reasons very instructive. Clifford said in that answer that it was quite true that we were not certain of the truth of the doctrine in question, but then, further, we were not certain of anything; and he contends that the evidence as to the descent of man is really as cogent as that for the descent of other animals. He argues this point with great ability. But the details of the argument are not our concern here. What we want to call attention to is the degree of certainty which Clifford claimed for the above doctrine as a whole. And it is important to notice this, because not only in the essay to which we are now alluding, but continually elsewhere throughout his works, we find him insisting on the extreme modesty of science, so different from the arrogance of theology. 'We must recollect,' he says, for instance, quoting Professor Huxley as an exponent of his own opinions, 'that any human belief, however broad its basis, however defensible it may seem, is, after all, only a probable belief.' And he is constantly asking us to notice how he always prefers to use the word 'probable' rather than 'certain.' But should anyone in this matter really take him at his word, and believe that practically there was the very least uncertainty either as to the truth of the above-mentioned doctrine or more particularly as to the descent of man, his answer, he informs us, would be this: 'Don't be so silly; I have no patience with you.' Indeed, as to his meaning, he is yet more explicit; and he tells us in so many words, that when our physicists modestly say they are not certain that man was descended from not-men, and that these not-men were descended from unconscious and inorganic matter, they mean that they are a great deal more certain of the fact than any of us can be as to the taking of Plevna by the Russians. They mean that they are more 'cock-sure' in their doubts than the generality of us are in our certainties.

Such in rough outline being Clifford's physical creed, and such the doubt or certainty with which he held and taught it, let us next consider his metaphysical creed, not forgetting how greatly it is to his credit that he saw the necessity for any metaphysical creed at all. He has arrived, let us remember, from the lifeless and uninhabited earth, at the human race, and at human consciousness; and now comes a question which, though historically it is the last, yet logically is the first of all. What is consciousness? or rather, What is knowledge? Unlike the majority of modern men of science, Clifford saw that the methods which are commonly called scientific, though they might rear up a vast superstructure of knowledge, yet left the foundations of it to take care of themselves, and that it was possible, unless these were looked to, to undermine them completely. He saw that all material analysis of the universe, all discoveries as to the connection of mind with brain, all theories of sight and of sensation, and the getting together and transmission of various kinds of knowledge, might, from one point of view be plausibly proved worthless, and be robbed of all the meaning they were supposed to have. Let us trace all existing things to atoms, and out of the movements of these atoms trace the formation of the body and brain of man, yet from one point of view we have made no advance whatever. The question still remains, what are these atoms? If from one point of view consciousness is produced by them, from another they are the creations of consciousness. If we can think of mind only in terms of matter, we can think of matter only in terms of mind, and it seems that outside our own consciousness nothing exists at all.

If I consider merely my own feelings (says Clifford), and ask what evidence they give of anything beyond them, it seems to me that I must answer no evidence at all. . . . If I say that such and such things existed at some previous time, I mean that, if I had been there, I could have perceived them. If I say that there is hydrogen in the sun, I mean that, if I could get any of that gas, I should be able to burn it in oxygen, and produce exactly the same impressions on my senses as those which, in the aggregate, I call water.

It is true that these words betray a certain vacillation of thought, which is not confined to this special passage. But they show us quite sufficiently that the initial problem in question was fully perceived by Clifford. If we say that an atom is the ultimate unit of things, we mean by an atom something that, were our senses fine enough, would exist for us as an individual feeling. And Clifford saw that it was needful to maintain science as something more than the analysis of the feelings of the individual. The progress of philosophy in this respect, Clifford said, began with Berkeley, 'who establshed, in a security that has never yielded to attack, the subjective character of the world of phenomena : that this world I perceive *is* my perceptions, and nothing more.' But besides these perceptions, said Berkeley, there is also a spirit, a *me* that perceives them. And 'to get rid,' says

Clifford, ' of this imaginary soul or substance was the work of Hume.' The next important step was made by Mill, who defined more completely the views of Hume, and explained by the law of association how we come to believe in the external world. After Mill came Mr. Herbert Spencer, who combined the analysis of mental action given by the association theory with ' the analysis of nervous action supplied by the histologists,' proving that the evolution of mind ' proceeds *pari passu* ' with the evolution of the organism.

Here, then (says Clifford) is the great advantage of Mr. Herbert Spencer in the study of both orders of facts. He can make any step in analysis of the one help in analysis of the other. And accordingly he has carried both to an extent that leaves all previous investigators far behind. But you will see at once that we must look at the question of idealism from the physiological point of view. And accordingly he considers that there *is* something different from our perceptions, the changes in which correspond in a certain way to the changes in the worlds we perceive. He thinks, however, we can never know what it is; and he says—' . . . The antithesis of subject and object, never to be transcended whilst consciousness lasts, renders impossible all knowledge of that ultimate reality in which subject and object are united.' . . . Mr. Spencer attempts to make my feelings give me evidence of something that is not included among them. A careful study of all his arguments to that effect has only convinced me over again that the attempt is hopeless.

Though Mr. Herbert Spencer has failed, Clifford tells us that he can himself succeed. 'Can we,' he says, 'get out of our hobble and arrive at real knowledge derived from external experience, from *messages*, and not from *imagination*? I think we can.' But our knowledge, he warns us, will be of the nature not of certainty, but of inference; and inference depends on a something that is not inferred itself. It depends upon one grand assumption, and that assumption is the uniformity of nature. And why, Clifford asks, do we assume that? 'I cannot,' he answers, 'give you a logical reason for believing it, but I can give you a physical explanation of the fact that we all do believe it. We believe,' he says—and it will be well to quote this passage *in extenso*—

we believe a thing when we are prepared to act as if it were true. Now, if you and I had not habitually acted on the assumption of the uniformity of nature from the time when we could act at all, we should not be here to discuss the question. Nature is selecting for survival those individuals and races who act as if she were uniform; and hence the gradual spread of that belief over the civilised world.

This uniformity may be merely a uniformity of *phenomena*, a law relating to my feelings. So long as I only am concerned, it seems to me that the idealist theory is perfectly sufficient. It is quite capable of explaining *me*, but when *you* come into the question it is perfectly at a loss. . . . I do believe that you are conscious in the same way that I am; and once that is conceded, the whole idealist theory falls to pieces. For there are feelings which are not my feelings, which are entirely outside my consciousness; so that there is at least an external world. But let us consider now in what way we infer it; why do I believe that there are feelings which are not mine? Because, as I belong to a gregarious race, the greater part of my life consists in acting upon the position that it is true.

Clifford wrote this as early as 1873; but the views just stated he seems never to have changed subsequently, though he invented, for the sake of accuracy, a new piece of terminology. 'Things presented in my consciousness, phenomena, I propose,' he says subsequently, 'to call *objects*, whilst *your* feelings, which are not, and cannot by any possibility become, objects in my consciousness,' but which 'are inferred, and in the very act of inference *thrown out* of my consciousness, recognised as outside of it, as *not* being a part of me, I propose to call *ejects*.' Making use of these terms, Clifford proceeds to point out how the belief in the existence of ejects profoundly modifies the object. He takes a table for instance, and shows how complex our conception is of it—how it is a conception of 'a table as an object in the minds of men . . . an indefinite number of ejects, together with one object, which the conception of each eject more or less resembles.' This complex conception he calls the 'social object,' and we gain the impression of its *externality* by this 'sub-conscious reference to supposed ejects.' But Clifford warns us not to think that our argument has brought us too far. Our impression of the 'outness' of the social object thus accounted for does not enable us to argue that there is anything 'outside of my consciousness except the minds of other men.' This all-important step yet demands to be taken. We arrive at this by observing 'the correspondence or parallelism between mind and body.' Mind, or consciousness, is an exceedingly complex thing. It is not a unit, as thinkers used to suppose. Mind, consciousness, or a sense of personality, consists of 'a stream of feelings so compact together that at each instant it consists of (1) new feelings, (2) fainter repetitions of previous ones, and (3) links connecting these repetitions.' Now we know from the highest scientific authorities that 'the complexity of consciousness is paralleled by complexity of action in the brain,' and there is reason to believe that 'as consciousness co-exists with complex brain motion, so elementary feeling co-exists with elementary brain motion.' From this, Clifford argues, it follows that elementary feeling does not imply consciousness, but that without consciousness 'a feeling can exist by itself' He continues thus :—

> If that doctrine be true, we shall have along the line of the human pedigree a series of imperceptible steps connecting inorganic matter with ourselves. To the later members of that series we must undoubtedly ascribe consciousness, although it must of course have been simpler than our own. . . . As we go back along the line, the complexity of the organism and of its nerve-action insensibly diminishes; and for the first part of our course we see reason to think that the complexity of consciousness insensibly diminishes also. But if we make a jump, say to the tunicate molluscs, we see no reason to infer the existence of consciousness at all. Yet not only is it impossible to point out a place where any sudden break takes place, but it is contrary to all the natural training of our minds to suppose a breach of continuity so great. . . . There is only one way out of the difficulty, and to that we are driven. . . . As the line of ascent is unbroken, and must end at last in inorganic matter, we have no choice but to admit that every motion of matter is simultaneous with some ejective fact or event, which might be a part of consciousness. . . . From this follow two important corollaries. (1) A feeling can exist by itself, without forming a part of consciousness. It does not depend for its existence on the consciousness of which it may form a part. Hence a feeling (or an eject-element) is a *Ding an sich*, an

absolute, whose existence is not relative to anything else. *Sentitur* is all that can be said. (2) These eject-elements, which correspond to motions of matter, are connected together in their sequence and co-existence by counterparts of the physical laws of matter. . . . That element then, (Clifford proceeds), of which, as we have seen, even the simplest feeling is a complex, I shall call *mind-stuff*. A moving molecule of inorganic matter does not possess mind or consciousness, but it possesses a small piece of mind-stuff . . . and, when matter takes the complex form of a living human brain, the corresponding mind-stuff takes the form of a human consciousness, having intelligence and volition. . . . The two chief points of this doctrine may be thus summed up :—Matter is a mental picture, in which mind-stuff is the thing represented. Reason, intelligence, and volition are properties of a complex which is made up of elements themselves not rational, not intelligent, not conscious.

So far as he was himself concerned, Clifford looked on this theory as his own; but he not only tells us that, after it dawned on him, he learned that several of his friends had arrived at something similar, but he adds, in another place, that it now was no mere guess or conjecture, but the view at which all the greatest thinkers had arrived and were arriving; and he intended to have included it in a book to be called ‘The Creed of Science.’

We will not at present pause to criticise, but will pass on first to the remaining parts of his system. Thus far he has derived living and conscious man from inanimate and unconscious matter, and has explained what that matter is, and the process of its transformation. If this account be true, it follows without saying that all knowledge is derived from experience, and cannot possibly have any other source—not the experience of the individual only, but the slowly acquired and transmitted experience of the race. Clifford saw, however, that there was one great difficulty in the way of this theory, and that was the necessity and the universality of the truths of geometry. Having spoken of the various ways in which these have been explained, 'it seems,' he says, 'to me that the Kantian dilemma about universal propositions is just as valid now, in spite of these explanations, as it was in his time. . . . Either I have some source of knowledge other than experience, and I must admit the existence of *à priori* truths, independent of experience; or I cannot know that any universal statement is true.' Now experience, Clifford says, *must* be the only source of knowledge, for if it were not, the evolution theory would be found inadequate; 'so that I am driven,' he continues, 'to conclude in regard to every apparently universal statement, either that it is not really universal . . . . or that I do not know that it is true.' He was well aware that this alternative presented many apparent difficulties, and that these were not to be removed without much intellectual labour. But the way out of them, he conceived, had been at last discovered by certain modern Continental speculators, whose opinions he embraced with enthusiasm. This school has sought to effect a complete revolution in our conception of geometrical truths. Its position is that these are neither necessarily nor universally true now, and that in the remoter past they may not have been true at all. There may be triangles whose angles do not equal two right angles; there may be converging parallel lines; there may be two straight lines that enclose a space The change in scientific ideas indicated by these startling doctrines is, says Clifford, 'of transcendent importance,' and for this reason: 'it is a change in our conception of the cosmos. Were the Euclidean assumptions true, the constitution of the universe, at an infinite distance from us, would be as well known as the geometry of this room . . . so that here we should have real knowledge of something at least that concerns the cosmos, something that is true throughout the immensities and the eternities. That something Lobatchewsky and his followers have taken away... The knowledge of immensity and eternity is replaced by a knowledge of Here and Now.' And thus, Clifford argued, we have no knowledge that the evolution theory will not account for, and, as a supposed corollary, we have no reason for believing in an immaterial soul, and no parallels by which to illustrate and support a belief in a theological intuition.

Let us now pass on to Clifford's doctrine of the human will. 'The mind,' he says, 'is to be regarded as a stream of feelings which runs parallel to, and is simultaneous with, the action of that particular part of the brain in which the cerebrum and the sensory tract are excited.' The body, of which the brain is a part, and on which its action is dependent, 'is a physical machine, which goes by itself according to a physical law, that is to say, is automatic. An automaton is a thing which goes by itself when it is wound up, and we go by ourselves when we have food.' Were other men not conscious, we might regard them as 'mere machines;' but, as a matter of fact, they are machines attended by consciousness—they are conscious automata. Clifford here anticipates the objections, that if we are automata, we have no freedom of will and no moral responsibility. But with both of these he makes short work indeed. So far from the doctrine of automatism, being a denial of the doctrine of free will, it is, he says, the only accurate expression of it. An automaton, he says, is the exact opposite of a puppet. A puppet requires to be pushed or pulled by wires, and an automaton goes by itself. People only object, Clifford thinks, to the doctrine of human automatism because they are thinking of automata that have been made by man with certain definite intentions, and whose whole action is determined by a person outside; but the race of human automata have collectively made themselves. And this, he says, puts the two cases on an entirely different footing. For the will to be free, we need no doctrine of the creation of energy in the brain; we need not believe that in the movements of the brain-molecules the uniformity of nature is even infinitesimally violated. If we want to know what free will is, says Clifford, Kant is the man to tell us; and free will, according to Kant, is that property which enables us to originate events independently of foreign determining causes; 'which, it seems to me,' proceeds Clifford, 'amounts to saying precisely that we are automata, that is, we go by ourselves, and do not want anybody to push or pull us.' With similar facility he goes on to show us that exactly the same conclusion is contained in the doctrine of responsibility. 'If,' he says, 'there is a certain point where the law of causation does not apply, where my action does not follow by regular physical causes from what I am, then I am not responsible for it, because it is not I that do it. So you see the notion that we are not automata destroys responsibility.' Clifford, however, does not end here, but adds this significant sentence :—

Moreover, if we once admit that physical causes are not continuous, but that there is some break, then we leave the way open for the doctrine of a destiny or a providence outside of us, overruling human efforts, and guiding human history to a foregone conclusion. ... I do think that if it is right to call any doctrine immoral, it is right so to call this doctrine, when we remember how often it has paralysed the efforts of those who were honestly climbing up the hillside towards the light and right, and how often it has nerved the sacrilegious arm of the fanatic or the adventurer who was conspiring against society.

E

Having carried our survey of Clifford's views thus far, we are now, as the above sentence may suggest to us, in a position to enter upon a new part of them—the historical. We include in history not those times only of which we have written records, but those times also which are sometimes called prehistoric; for in these were first shaped the beginnings of that society against which the fanatics of theism have so often conspired, and we can understand society only by a study of the first beginnings of it. Thus out of historical knowledge springs directly ethical knowledge, or the knowledge of right and wrong. It is the opinion of Clifford's school that up to a very recent date the whole civilised world has been in error on these matters—completely in error theoretically, and in very grave error practically. The cause of this confusion has been the theories of theology, which represented ethics as resting on a completely false foundation; and this confusion it is that Clifford's school have undertaken to dispel. For the source, it tells us, of our moral rules and obligations we must look to no superhuman lawgiver. Morality is nothing if not human. It is nothing but the necessary cause, accompaniment, and condition of the gradual evolution of society. It is, in other words, the condition of co-operation; and co-operation has been imperative on man for two reasons—first, because of the struggle for existence; secondly, because men are gregarious animals. The human struggle for existence was at first not a struggle of individual against individual so much as a struggle of tribe against tribe. The original savage, says Clifford, being little able to reflect, was probably not possessed clearly of the conception of his individual self. He was, however, preyed upon perpetually by unreflecting and immediate desires; and thus his conception of self was not only less used and developed, 'but was also,' says Clifford, 'less definite and more wide.' He found that the satisfaction of his immediate desires depended on the strength and the well-being of his tribe; and thus this external object, his tribe, became associated with all his pains and pleasures, and was identified by him with himself. 'Now the tribe,' says Clifford, '*quâ* tribe, has to exist, and it can only exist by aid of such an organic artifice as the conception of the tribal self in the minds of its members. Hence the natural selection of those races in which this conception is most powerful.' But, along with this kind of primeval progress, something else also was in process of development ; and that was the conception of the individual self, not as identified with the tribal self, but as distinguished from it. Thus gradually there were developed in the individual two rival selves, each of which 'became fixed as a specific character in the constitution of social man.' The quality or disposition in an individual which gives his individual self the supremacy we now know under the common name of selfishness ; while the quality or disposition which gives his tribal self the supremacy is called by Clifford *piety*. Man had by this time grown a more or less civilised being ; and his actions had lost much of their instinctive character, and had become to a great extent calculating and deliberate. The result of this progress was to increase the power of selfishness as the rival of piety, and to produce what we now know as the conscious moral struggle. Piety, therefore, says Clifford, had to be 'encouraged,' and it was encouraged by 'the common approbation of individual acts,' regarded as good for the community ; and natural selection in the long run has preserved those tribes which have approved of the right things—namely, those things which at that time gave the tribe an advantage in the struggle for existence.

And now (says Clifford) let us take the man who habitually does such things as are advantageous for the tribe. Such a man the tribe cannot fail to approve of; and the pious or tribal self of each member of the tribe says to such a man 'I like you.' This is moral approbation. But let us take another case. Let us suppose a man has done something that is obviously harmful to the tribe, owing to his selfishness having got the better of his piety. By-and-by his piety reasserts itself, and the man says 'In the name of the tribe, I do not like this thing that I, as an individual, have done.' . . . This self-judgment in the name of the tribe, Clifford proceeds, is called Conscience. If the man goes farther and draws from this act an inference about his own character, he may say 'In the name of the tribe, I do not like my individual self.' This is Remorse. . . . In a mind sufficiently developed to distinguish the individual from the tribal self, conscience is thus a necessary result of the existence of piety; it is ready to hand as a means for its increase.

Thus far, however, Clifford admits that he has only accounted for conscience in its elemental form. If we wish to understand the present moral nature of man, we must consider how society has used the feelings of the individual as a means for its own preservation. In our present state of development the moral sense has become purely intuitive; conscience gives us imperative orders, assigning no reasons. Now how has this come about? It has come about in this way. Conscience in the individual, at this stage of man's development, represents not the experience and wisdom of the individual, but the inherited wisdom of the tribe, which has been ingrained in the individual, not only through natural selection and the survival of the fittest, but by the two following processes, of which one is direct and the other indirect. If a man offends, the tribe may directly express its disapproval by killing the man, or inflicting on him some material punishment; or else it may punish him indirectly, by pouring out its anger and contempt upon his selfishness, until his own pious self takes part with the tribal judgment, and endorses the condemnation that is thus passed upon him. Finally, to these processes we must add a third, which is a union of the former two. 'Self-judgment,' says Clifford, 'in the name of the tribe, becomes associated with very definite and material judgment by the tribe itself;' and thus the motive power of conscience is 'strengthened to an enormous degree,' and its decisions are guided and made definite by the definite nature and occasion of the public penalty.

Such, then, is the natural history of the growth of conscience, which Clifford thinks amply sufficient to explain it in its present condition. And from this explanation of it he thinks we arrive at a clear notion of what we mean by moral responsibility. We are morally responsible, he says, 'when we can be punished for doing wrong, with approval of the tribal self,' be the punishment either our own self-condemnation or the condemnation or the punishment of us by others. And 'responsibility,' says Clifford, implies two things—(1) 'The act was a product of the man's character and of the circumstances, and his character may to a certain extent be inferred from the act; (2) the man had a conscience which might have been so worked upon as to prevent him committing the act.'

And now comes the grand conclusion to which the above views lead us. The old conception of virtue was an entirely wrong one. It was not only not the truth, but the direct denial of the truth. According to the old theory, we were to be virtuous, because we owed a debt to ourselves or to the God who made us, and for whose sake we were bound to keep ourselves pure. But according to the new theory we owe ourselves nothing. Self-improvement, as self-improvement, is a vice, and not a virtue.

> There are (says Clifford) no self-regarding virtues. The qualities of courage, prudence, &c., can only be *rightly* encouraged in so far as they are shown to conduce to the efficiency of the citizen; that is, in so far as they cease to be self-regarding. The duty of private judgment, of searching after truth, the sacredness of belief which ought not to be misused on unproved statements, follow only on showing of the enormous importance to society of a true knowledge of things. And any diversion of conscience from its sole allegiance to the community, is condemned *à priori* in the very nature of right and wrong.

Such being the case, Clifford looked on what is commonly called history—that is, such history as is derived from written records—as the above philosophy teaching by example. For him such history was the history of the true view of things, obscured by superstition and misconception—sometimes more obscured and sometimes less—and ever struggling to break through what obscured it. So far as in the present volumes he appeals to past events, he appeals to them only to bear him out in his ethical and non-religious theories, and to show that these at last are gaining their final victory, and are ushering in a new era. And what is the result? Clifford was prepared to tell us.

> The dim and shadowy outlines (he says) of the superhuman deity fade slowly away from before us; and as the mist of his presence floats aside we perceive with greater and greater clearness the shape of a yet grander and nobler figure—of Him who made all gods and shall unmake them. From the dim dawn of history, and from the inmost depth of every soul, the face of our father Man looks out upon us with the fire of eternal youth in his eyes, and says, '*Before* JEHOVAH *was*, I AM!'

And now let us enquire finally what Clifford's practical preaching was to this new age which he conceived himself, amongst others, to be inaugurating. What was it that he tried to make the men about him do, and that he concluded they would do? In the first place, as we have seen already, he said to them: Don't think about saving your own souls. They are nothing to you. Don't think about any duties to a superhuman deity, for there is no such being, and, even if there were, you could have no duties towards him. These two beliefs have been the source of half the evil that is in the world. In the second place he said to them:

Instead of your own souls and your God, you must put society. At present you must put the special community to which you happen to belong, and by-and-by, when you grow more and more instructed, you must learn to include in that community all the human race. And how are you to serve the community? and what is to be the result of your service? You are to serve it by striving after 'increased efficiency, each of you in your special work as well as in the social functions which are common to you all. You must strive each of you to be a better citizen, a better workman, a better son, husband, or father.' And if you do this, all of you, the community of which you are each of you a part will through all the coming generations grow healthier and better; it will go from strength to strength, and will by-and-by reach heights of which we have hardly a conception.

The progress of the community, then, being the end of all individual action, how are we of this generation to adapt our means to the end? 'Such adaptation,' says Clifford, 'may be produced in two ways that we at present know of—by processes of natural selection, and by the agency of an intelligence in which an image or

idea of the end preceded the use of the means.'
Now, natural selection is the work of nature.
The individual teacher has nothing to do with
that. His sole concern lies with the intelligence
of those he addresses. And not only is it this
only that he can work upon, but it is this that
for the future must be the chief force at work.
Progress hitherto has been largely unconscious.
Men thought indeed they were going in one
direction, but natural causes have been really
taking them in another. But now a change has
come. The world is being baptised into a new
life. The real meaning of the moral sense is at
last discovered, 'and it must,' says Clifford, 'be
directed for the future by our conscious discovery of the tribal purpose which it serves.'
'Conscience,' he repeats again, 'is the voice of
man within us commanding us to work for man.'
And thus the work of the preacher and the
teacher is twofold; he has in the first place to
direct this conscience, and in the next place he
has to strengthen it, and to give force to its
mandates.

Clifford's premature death has, of course,
left his practical teaching incomplete. He has
indeed accomplished with sufficient clearness the

first of the two tasks just mentioned, but he hardly had time to do more than touch explicitly on the second. He has told us that the great work of each of us is to make our piety overcome our selfishness, and that the object of our piety is the social organism. But how this piety for the future is to be strengthened in its hard struggle with its enemy he has only given us hints here and there by the way. His views, however, on this matter we can arrive at pretty clearly, and of all his views they are perhaps the most significant. We will speak of them presently; but first of all let us look back on the other parts of his system, the main outlines of which we have now glanced at.

It is true that in these there is nothing that, at the present time, can be very new or startling to any of us. But, as assimilated and expressed by Clifford, we have thought the modern system well worth considering. Amongst our scientific thinkers he was a man of unusual culture, as well as of unusual ability; and the weakness of the theories he advocated, and the insufficiency of the training he had received, are best visible in a man who naturally was so highly gifted.

Of his views on physical science there is obviously no need to speak. He was simply here an intelligent disciple of others, whom we have no call to criticise. But what we do propose to examine is the methods by which he proposed to place this physical science on a firm philosophic basis, and to reconcile its teachings with the verdicts of our moral consciousness. And first let us consider how he deals with the first of all questions—the existence of an external world. Its existence as we have seen he conceived he had established, and that he had set right on this point all former philosophers, from Berkeley to Herbert Spencer. And it must be admitted that in his views and in the exposition of them there are displayed great ingenuity and great power of thought. But when we come to examine the final upshot of them, we shall find that they all end in nothing. He succeeds with extreme skill in travelling round a circle, and in the end he finds himself just where he started. And, curiously enough, in two places he virtually admits this himself. We can only, he maintains, free ourselves from the position of absolute idealism by our belief in what he calls 'personal ejects;'

and why, he asks, does he believe in these? why does he believe that there are feelings which are not his own? 'Because,' he answers, 'as I belong to a gregarious race, the greater part of my life consists in acting upon the supposition that it is true.' This is literally the only answer that he gives to the great question; and he gives this not hastily, but with all deliberation, and he leads solemnly up to it, as a piece of profound wisdom. Now what does this sentence amount to? To believe that there are feelings which are not his own is the same thing as to believe that he belongs to a race. The question, then, that he is really asking is, 'Why do I believe that I belong to a race?' And his only answer is, 'Because I belong to a gregarious race.' But this is not all. In another place precisely the same question is again asked by him, and what he says there is very different and far more to the purpose. 'How,' he says, 'this inference is justified, how consciousness can testify to anything outside itself, I do not pretend to say. I need not untie a knot that the world has cut for me long ago. . . . The position of absolute idealism may therefore be left out of count, although each individual may be unable to justify his dissent from it.' Now let us suppose this last statement true, and we have one thing to observe that Clifford seems altogether to have forgotten. It may be quite true that the belief in question is not only inexplicable, but indubitable ; but we by no means have disposed of it by admitting that. According to Clifford's philosophy all knowledge is based on experience ; if he cannot maintain that position, his whole system falls to the ground ; and here we find him, apparently quite unconscious of the results of it, not admitting only but proclaiming that the one fact of our daily life, on our knowledge of which all other knowledge is based, is a fact that no experience could have taught us, and that we must have learned it from some other source.

It is true that, granting the existence of the personal eject, Clifford deduces with much ingenuity from it the existence of ejects that are not personal—in other words, the inorganic universe. But here again, in spite of all his skill, his reasonings prove useless. They depend, as we have seen already, upon his theory of the nature of things in themselves. And what does this theory amount to ? Ingenious as are the means by which he arrives at his results, the results when arrived at are crude and puerile to an almost inconceivable degree. 'The thing in itself' is, he tells us, elementary feeling, mind-stuff, or quasi-mind; and this is known to us as matter. With every moving molecule of matter there moves also a small particle of mind-stuff which is attached to it. Now, not only must it be obvious to anyone at all trained in philosophical thinking that this theory leaves time, and still more plainly space, entirely unaccounted for; but there is a further and yet more obvious objection to it, which has not escaped even his own enthusiastic biographer. This theory, which Clifford flattered himself was a new form of monism, is in reality nothing but the dualism it was intended to replace; only he chooses to call matter 'mind-stuff,' and he chooses to call mind 'consciousness.' His theory, he tells us, rests on the doctrine that there can be feeling without consciousness, a statement to which it is impossible to affix any meaning whatsoever. The old-fashioned dualism was the statement of a mystery, but it was the statement of it in intelligible language. Clifford transferred the mystery from the statement to the way of stating it; and instead of simplifying a fact, he merely made his language meaningless.

But the confusion in his philosophy becomes most apparent, and is of most practical importance, when he comes to treat of mind and body in connection with human automatism and the freedom of the will. It would be hard to imagine, were the fact not before our eyes, that any man of Clifford's powers should have shown himself, on a point like this, so utterly incapable of clear and coherent thought, or of seeing steadily for a moment what is the real point at issue. As a specimen of his philosophical manner, we may first notice how he prepares the ground for himself. 'The will,' he says, 'is not a material thing. It is not a mode of material motion. Such an assertion belongs to the crude materialism of the savage. The only thing that influences matter is the position of surrounding matter, or the motion of surrounding matter;' and thus he lays down, as if to close the question for ever, 'if anybody says that the will influences matter, the statement is not untrue, but it is nonsense. . . . It is a combination of words whose corresponding ideas will not go together.'

F

Anything more utterly false, and we may add foolish, than this, it is not easy to imagine. That will should influence matter may or may not be a possibility; but it is the expression of a distinct belief, and of a belief that is held by a very large number of people. One important example of it is the belief that God orders the world; and Clifford not only holds that to this proposition a very distinct idea can attach itself, but an idea that is so powerful as to be of the utmost practical danger. There is another answer to him that is even more near to hand. He says that to say matter influences will is not untrue but nonsense. But let us take the converse of this proposition; and that, as he would be the first to admit, is not only not nonsense, but it is true. Give a man wine, and you nerve his will to fight. Give a man more wine, and you put his will to sleep for a time. Stab him in the heart with a dagger, and you extinguish his will for ever.

It is perfectly true, however, to say, that for will to influence matter is, on Clifford's theory, impossible. On that theory, consciousness is nothing but a passive spectator, and the will itself is nothing but a fiction. The strange thing is, that Clifford himself neither admitted nor saw this, but thought he could show, on the contrary, not only that will was a reality, but also that it was free. And this brings us to the climax of his philosophical confusions. 'That man is a free agent appears to me obvious, and that in the natural sense of the words. We need ask for no better definition than Kant's: "Will is a kind of causality belonging to living agents, in so far as they are rational; and freedom is such a property of causality as enables them to be efficient agents independently of outside causes determining them; as, on the other hand, necessity is that property of all irrational beings which consists in their being determined to activity by the influence of outside causes."' Now this, no doubt, at first sight sounds well enough; but it seems to have escaped Clifford that these words of Kant belonged to one philosophy, and that in being transplanted to another they become nonsense. We need not pause to point out that, in the first place, will, in Clifford's system, is emphatically not a kind of causality at all. All we need remark upon is the use of the words 'outside causes.' Now, according to Clifford, an outside cause is any cause outside 'my consciousness;' and if there is one thing that his theory teaches more plainly than another, it is that men cannot be 'efficient agents independently of outside causes;' nay, more than this, they cannot be agents at all. 'I believe,' says Clifford, 'that I am a free agent, when my actions are independent of the circumstances outside me.' But this, according to his theory, no man's actions ever are. So far from our being independent of such circumstances, we are entirely at the mercy of them; we are like 'all irrational beings,' as described by Kant; 'we are determined to activity by the influence of outside causes.' In fact, the distinction between outside cause and any other kind of cause is here a wholly false one. Clifford says we are free because 'we go of ourselves, we do not want anybody to push or pull us.' Now of course, in a certain sense, we 'go of ourselves,' just as a tree does; but the direction in which we go, if it cannot be said to be determined by anyone pulling us, is determined by countless other things attracting us; and so far as freedom goes, and so far as *outsideness* in the matter goes, there is nothing to choose really between propulsion and attraction. I place three children on a stage, telling them not to move of themselves, but to allow me to push and pull them as I please, and then make them perform certain evolutions. The children, in so far as these movements are concerned, are merely marionettes or puppets. Clifford himself would have maintained that they were not free agents. Supposing, however, I knew the nature of the children sufficiently well, I could, by a certain arrangement of sweetmeats or other attractive objects about the stage, produce exactly the same movements, and I should be able to predict them with exactly the same certainty. The children in both cases would have been equally at my mercy; nor would it make the least difference in the present argument whether the cause that determined them to activity were my hand or a sugar-plum. That there is an accidental difference between the two cases is true enough, but the difference is only an accidental one. The action is in one case accompanied by the feeling which we call volition, and in the other case it is not. According to Clifford and his school, there are really but two kinds of action, each of them equally inevitable and equally necessary—action in which we are propelled, and action in which we are attracted; and what Clifford means by will, or by free will,[1] is nothing but the consciousness of being attracted, not propelled.

From this subject we pass to one directly connected with it, to the conscience and moral responsibility; and we shall find that precisely the same confusion exists in Clifford's mind here. 'In order,' he says, 'that a man may be morally responsible for an action, three things are necessary:—(1) He might have done something else; that is to say, the action was not wholly determined by external circumstances, and he is responsible only for the choice which was left him. (2) He had a conscience. (3) The action was one in regard to the doing or not doing of which conscience might have been a sufficient motive.' Now, from our point of view, all this is completely true; but that point of view is not Clifford's. All through this there runs a conception that in Clifford's system is totally inadmissible. He is perpetually presupposing the presence of some mysterious force whose

---

[1] According to Clifford's theory, to call the will free is only a piece of tautology. In the only sense in which the will is ever free, it is always free.

existence he has already denied—some force that need not follow the uniformity of nature—some *fatis avolsa potestas*. He betrays this in his use of the words 'might have been.' But in his system such a mood of the verb has no place at all. Nothing might have been but the things that have been; and were it not for the limitation of our own knowledge of details, we should see that it was as absurd to say a man might have acted otherwise than he did act, as to say that a stream might flow up a hill.

Still, however this may be, it will be said, and said truly, that conscience is a fact, and the sense of responsibility is a fact; that no theories can take them away; and that, by the bestowal of praise and blame, the conscience may be trained, just as a warped piece of timber may be straightened, so as to be of better service in the future no matter what our views are as to what might have been in the past. But even here the old difficulty clings to us; for, useful as moral blame might be, we shall see that the above view of things must, if it were ever fully adopted by us, completely paralyse our powers of blaming. Clifford says very truly that our right, or, in other words, our ability, to award blame, is in proportion to the presence or the absence of extenuating circumstances. When a man, for instance, has so strong an inclination to drink that we cannot conceive any conscience strong enough to overmaster it, he is not any more responsible for drinking than he would be for coughing if his glottis were irritated. 'But if it is not inconceivable,' says Clifford, 'that a very strong conscience fully brought to bear might succeed in conquering the inclination, we take a lenient view of the fall, but we shall still regard it as a fall, and say that the man is responsible.' Now between the two classes of actions which Clifford means to indicate there is indeed a difference; but he has quite misconceived its nature. The difference has no reference to the past or to what might have been, but to the future and what we conceive will be. According to Clifford's theory, we are not justified in blaming a man because he has acted in one way when he might have acted in another, but because, if we blame him for what he has done, he will be less likely to offend in the same way again. If we adopt this view, however, there is one point to remember. The blame in this case would be as desirable and as beneficial as in the other, but we shall find ourselves unable to award it. As Clifford himself tells us, blame diminishes as extenuating circumstances multiply; and, on Clifford's theory of human action, every offence has not only extenuating circumstances but circumstances that are completely exculpating. It is impossible for the worst of men to commit an action which the best of men under like circumstances would not have committed likewise.

We might dwell, did space permit us, on certain further results of the theory we are now considering. We might show how the logical result of it must be, that, if we are any of us responsible for anything, we are responsible not for our own sins, but for the sins of others, and that of those others the two most important parts are our fathers who are dead and our children who are unborn. But this particular matter would involve a long discussion as to the meaning of words and the associations they carry with them. It is more to our present purpose to note what we were before speaking of—the way in which Clifford has confused the perception that a thing would be desirable with the assumption that it would be possible; for it is this confusion that is most typical of his school, and which runs through all their more immediate preaching as to general human action, and through all their prophecies as to the future that is before humanity.

This leads us to approach the matter from a slightly different point of view. The end and object of our existence is, we have seen, to promote the progress of the community, and this progress is to be effected through the education and the intensification of the conscience. Clifford, it will be seen, here agrees with Mr. Herbert Spencer. Conscience, as conceived of by him, is an inherited tribal instinct traversing the individual appetites. Its voice is an instinctive voice, and its biddings, as Clifford expressly says, do not rest, in the individual, upon their true reasons. But what he and his school propose to do is to alter this state of things; they propose to make conscience rest its biddings on their true reasons, and guide them 'by a conscious discovery of the tribal purpose it serves.' But they forget that in doing this they are putting conscience in an entirely new position. Its instinctive character disappears; nay, more, as conscience it ceases to exist. It resolves itself into the ordinary intellectual judgment as to the means towards an end, the end in this case being presupposed the most desirable. And thus the problem for the prophets of progress is not how to strengthen conscience, but it is simpler and more direct. It is how to strengthen our conscious devotion to the community, so as to make it more and more dominant over our conscious devotion to ourselves.

And it is the difficulty and even the nature of this problem that Clifford and his school seem entirely to overlook. They imagine that their system will leave them the old power of conscience intact, and that the changes of view that they introduce will only add to it. But they forget one thing. They are right, on their own grounds, in calling conscience instinctive, inasmuch as its biddings do not rest on their true reasons; but they do rest on reasons, even though the reasons be not true. It is only through an assignment of reasons, through a statement of facts, and the drawing a conclusion from them, that conscience has the smallest power of enforcing its orders. This reasoning may be sometimes more articulate, and sometimes less, but it is always there; and one of the propositions contained in it is a personal menace to the individual. It not only gives an order, but it gives a curse or a blessing, and of one or other of these it foretells the sure fulfilment. It is, as Cardinal Newman has said, not only a king, but a prophet and a priest likewise. The truth of this statement, be it remembered, is quite independent of any theological doctrine. As a doctrine it may be true or false, but it certainly is true as an analysis of what conscience has been felt to be by the common consciousness of the mass of conscientious men. Now, according to Clifford's theory, conscience must be powerless as a king, and an impostor as a priest and a prophet. All its influence is, in fact, founded on a false prestige; and what Clifford and his school have fondly and foolishly imagined is that they can destroy the prestige and yet retain the power. They imagine they can remove the fulcrum, and yet employ the lever.

The same singular oversight, the same inability to grasp one entire side of the question, is to be found even more plainly when Clifford deals with Christianity as a fact in the history of progress. The Jews, he informs us, were ar eminently conscientious race, because of the difficulties with which, as a tribe, they had to contend in the struggle for existence; and that struggle was successful because their conscience was rightly informed.

> The moral teaching of Christ (says Clifford), . . . is the expression of the conscience of a people who had fought long and heroically for their national existence. In that long and terrible conflict they had learnt the supreme and overwhelming importance of conduct, . . . the weakness and uselessness of solitary and selfish efforts, the necessity for a man who would be a man to lose his poor single personality in the being of a greater and nobler combatant—the nation. And they said all this, after their fashion of short and potent sayings, perhaps better than any other men have said it before or since. It was this heroic people that produced the morality of the Sermon on the Mount.

This morality it is that is the one thing of value in Christianity; and this Clifford is confident that the world will go on practising with ever-increasing diligence. But of how the world has been induced to practise it in the past he says nothing, he thinks nothing. The importance of the part played by the ideal of Christ—of a Christ either divine or deified, an object at once of love, of worship, and of imitation—seems to have altogether escaped him. Study of history, observation of life, and ordinary common sense, seem alike to have left one half of his mind a complete blank; and whilst speculating on what would be good, if men were to do it, he has forgotten to consider for a moment what it is likely that men will do.

As a parallel to his above account of the origin of Christianity, we may mention his account of the Reformation in England, which is equally ludicrous in the ignorance and the naïve arrogance it betrays. The cause of the event in question was, he says, simple and single. It was none other than our great characteristic as Englishmen; it was 'the principle which forbids the priest to come between a man and his conscience.' Any statement more utterly false than this it is hardly possible to imagine. The English Reformation, as every schoolboy knows, was at first a political event, not a religious one; and the hatred of priests as priests, so far from being a cause of it, was only a late and a long-delayed result. Mr. Pollock himself is obliged to admit that Clifford studied history poetically, not scientifically. We should ourselves prefer to say that he studied it in the spirit of prejudice rather than in the spirit of poetry; and, when we say that the examples we have just adduced are fair, if not favourable, specimens of his historical criticism, the verdict will hardly be thought unjust. On whatever period he touches, his treatment of it is the same. Nor, when we consider his case, is this much to be wondered at. Of historical knowledge he had evidently only smatterings, and even these were fragmentary and disconnected; and he went to these smatterings, as he himself almost acknowledges, with the determination to make them bear witness to foregone conclusions, of which the most important was that all goodness was of purely human origin, and that the chief enemies of goodness were priesthoods generally, and the Christian priesthood in particular. We are far from attributing such a procedure to any dishonesty in Clifford's mind, but wonder certainly arises that to an honest man such a procedure should have been possible. The answer to this is to be found, we think, in that fault of Clifford and his school we were just now indicating, their utter want of any practical knowledge of human nature. Men and women, with all their complex motives, were not, to Clifford, realities. Simple, upright, and prejudiced in a certain way himself, he imagined that the great mass of human kind would be simple, upright, and prejudiced, just as he was. And the little esoteric ambitions and contempts of the common-room or the lecture hall, he mistook for the emotions and aspirations of the human kind in general.

And this is what we meant when we said that Clifford's teaching was to be best understood through his biography. Not only, as we have seen already, will his theory of things not hold together for a moment, but it is utterly unfit for any practical application. Considering Clifford's genius, such a result is singular; but we conceive it to be explained thus. Clifford's views of life and his desires to influence men were not what they were because he was an accurate thinker or a student of science or of philosophy; they were what they were because he came of the Christian middle class of England, and because every thought and every feeling he possessed was steeped in the beliefs and the sentiments of that class; and when he tells us about the nobleness of humanity and the grandeur of our Father Man, the emotions expressed are not the result of his scientific observations or of his later experiences, but they are the echo or the survival of emotions that had been ingrained in him at his mother's knee or under the arches of Exeter Cathedral. Clifford, as a practical preacher, as a dealer with his brother men, differed little in his knowledge and his feelings from an ordinary Bible-reader. What he did differ in from the Bible-reader was that the latter retains the original theoretical framework of his feelings; whereas Clifford had removed this, and was obliged to supply another. That he failed to see how unsound that other was theoretically, and how inefficient practically, can be explained also by an appeal to his life. His feelings seem, in reality, to have been the thing that guided him ; he was determined that his non-theistic theories should support these, and therefore any non-theistic theory that seemed to support them he was ready to accept as sound. Whilst as to the practical side of the question, just as his bringing up had made him deeply religious, and had left his morality, when his religion went, strongly touched with emotion, so had it left him unversed in the ways of the world at large ; and whilst endowing him with what, as a private character, we must call a beautiful innocence, it had left him in what,

G

as a public teacher, we must call a fatal ignorance.

If what we have said applied to Clifford only, it would hardly perhaps have been worth saying ; but, as we have observed already, it applies not to Clifford only, but to the whole modern school. If, as many think, that school is a really formidable foe to religion, it will be at any rate some comfort to know that it will certainly not destroy religion by replacing it. Its prestige, further, will be rendered less formidable if we reflect on how one of its best instructed and most gifted spokesmen has exhibited himself in these two volumes as hopelessly untrained in philosophy, hopelessly ill-read in history, and without the smallest grasp of that refractory human character of which he boasts that in the future his school will have the sole guidance.

TENNYSON'S BALLADS AND POEMS.[1]

To all admirers of Mr. Tennyson's genius his last volume should be one of singular interest; and this for two reasons. It not only claims our best attention for itself, but it turns our attention even more forcibly to its author. It throws a new light on his whole position and history, and at once helps and incites us to reconsider them. The poems comprised in it are of unequal merit and importance; but their strength and weakness in this way are both alike instructive. By-and-by we shall speak of them more in detail. It will be enough at present to make a brief allusion to one of them —the single poem of 'Rizpah.' Of this astonishing production it has been well said, that were all the rest of the author's works destroyed, this alone would at once place him amongst the first of the world's poets. Such was the verdict

[1] Ballads and Poems. By Alfred Tennyson. London: 1880.

pronounced by Mr. Swinburne. It has all his characteristic generosity, and hardly anything of his characteristic exaggeration.

Now to many men whose opinions are worth considering, an event of this kind must have been quite out of their calculations. It has been thought by many that, for a number of years past, Mr. Tennyson's powers have been more or less declining; and the decline they date probably from the publication of 'Enoch Arden.' With this view of the matter we do not ourselves agree, but we by no means hold it groundless. We hold, on the contrary, that it embodies an important truth, but a truth apprehended in a false and confused way. It is this confusion, we think, that the present volume will dissipate; in what manner we shall endeavour to show presently.

Of many men of genius it may be said truly that their powers declined towards the latter years of their lives, and in some cases altogether left them. Not to go far afield, we need think but of Scott and Southey, or of Swift, who 'expired a driveller and a show.' Here we have instances of a certain decline of powers, which, in a larger or less degree, is no unusual thing; and when it has been said of a genius that his powers showed signs of failing him, it has been meant generally, and probably meant truly, that a certain change had taken place in his brain. There are other cases, however, in which similar signs occur, but the cause to which they are due is altogether different. It is external, it is not internal. No change is involved in the brain of the man in question. His powers may still exist in all their earlier vigour. What does not exist as it once did is the earlier stimulus to use them. The powers of some men, for instance, have been mainly roused by poverty, those of others by ambition; and with the achievement either of fame or riches the powers have not decayed, they have only been employed languidly. Mr. Tennyson's case, we conceive, is analogous in one way to these. We do not mean that either fame or wealth has affected in any degree the exercise of his genius, but that the cause that has affected it is equally external. It is not in him, it is without him. His last volume must convince us that his vigour is unimpaired. His sight is not dim, nor his bodily strength abated. We may compare him to a mirror reflecting the sky's light on us, which was once dazzling, but which has slowly been growing dimmer; and the cause we shall find to be not that the mirror is tarnished, but one very different —that the sun is sinking.

We have not chosen this last image at random. The days have long gone by since the man of genius was looked upon as a kind of mysterious aerolite fallen to earth from heaven, and connected with his surroundings in only an accidental way. He is recognised now as the special outcome of his age; and he is conditioned by its conditions, even while he assists to change them. This remark will apply to all genius, but we are speaking now with a special view to the poet's. The poet is, as it were, at once a mirror and a burning-glass. He receives the light and the images that are round him; he intensifies the one, and he reduces the other to order: but the spectrum of this reflected world still depends on the actual world it reflects. This is true even of those poets who are said to be most original. The word *original* indeed, in this connexion, has been a source of great confusion, and it still serves to perpetuate an entirely false conception. It is supposed commonly to be a word of the highest praise when applied to a poet's genius, and the judgment conveyed by it seems to amount to this—that the poet's chief ideas spring from himself alone, and that he has not acquired or chosen them from any external source. Now the truth is, that could this be said with accuracy of any ideas at all, it could be said not of the greatest, but only of the most contemptible; and if we use the word in question with the meaning above referred to, we shall find more originality in the eccentricities of a baby than we shall in the pages of a Shakespeare. The sources of the highest poetry are, on the contrary, essentially external, and often borrowed from that which has preceded the poet or from that which surrounds him. Nor is this true only of plots and of constructions; it is true also of thoughts, and true in a deeper way. The great thoughts of the world have always matured slowly; they have never sprung full-grown from the head of any Thunderer; and when they have burst on an age as new from the lips of any poet, they have been thoughts that were already existing, only existing unrecognised. The poet has evoked them from the age, he has not added them to it.

And is this all, it may perhaps be asked—is this all that the greatest poets do for us? We answer that this is far more than it seems to be. We have compared the poet to a mirror, we have compared his works to a reflection; but the mirror and the reflection are both of a special kind. What is shown us is an image of the common world we live in, but it is not that world as common eyes see it. Spirits are reflected as well as bodies; bodies themselves become half-transparent. As we look our eyes are opened, the invisible is revealed to us, we are shown our own existence under new and unexpected aspects. The hopes, and thoughts, and doubts that have been hovering in the air around us, troubling all of us and eluding all of us, have been compelled by the poet to put on fitting bodies—to assume a 'questionable shape.' What the poet does is to reveal an epoch to itself. No poet can do more than this; only the greatest poets can do so much. But more is comprised in this than there may at first sight seem to be. In the vulgar sense no great thoughts may be original, but practically the man may be well said to originate them who makes them arrrange and show themselves, who confronts the age with its own image, and who points its aspirations to the goal they have been dimly seeking for.

If this be accepted as the great poet's function, we shall realise two points as to the great poet's genius. We shall realise first how great that genius has to be. The poet's mind can reflect those things only with which it is itself in sympathy, and, to reflect the character of an age, it must be in sympathy with many things. It must have grasped the science and the philosophy by which the intellect of the age is either ruled or agitated; it must have the same grasp on religious and political feeling. These requirements must be remembered, and how great these requirements are. But there is something more besides. We must remember that be the genius never so great, it can grasp and assimilate nothing but what is present for it to assimilate; and that its nature, be it what it will, is subdued to what it works in.

We have been led into making the above remarks because, in a singularly clear way, Mr. Tennyson is an illustration of the truth of them. In his poetry, more clearly than in that of most poets, we can recognise his own age reflected, and perceive the real relation between art and nature; indeed, from a study of his more mature poems one might almost construct the spiritual and even the political history of his epoch. That such a history would be complete we do not say. It is given to no one man to understand his own epoch completely, and there are doubtless forces at work in the world at present that have eluded Mr. Tennyson. To say this is not to disparage his genius. What he has failed to do does but show that he is not greater than the greatest men; what he has done shows that he is very nearly their equal. The more we study his best and sincerest works, the more shall we realise how wide have been his sympathies, how varied his knowledge, and how firm has been his grasp of whatever matter he has mastered. The speculative philosophy, the scientific knowledge of his age; the bearings of these upon religion, and the bearings of religion upon conduct; the passions of a people either for peace or war, for order or for liberty; the dark and the bright side of civilisation and material progress; the self-assertion of the people as against the claims of birth and privilege; and again the claims of culture, and the sense of *noblesse oblige*—all these has Mr. Tennyson understood and assimilated. In his powers of understanding and sympathy he is many-minded, not only many-sided. He is not one man, but a set of men. He is at once metaphysician and physicist, sceptic, and theologian, democrat and aristocrat, radical and royalist, fierce patriot and far-seeing cosmopolitan; and he has revealed to the age the strange interaction of these varied characters, and how the beliefs and the passions of each modify and are modified by those of all the others.

If we will but bear in mind Mr. Tennyson's relation to his age, and the history of that age during the past thirty-five years of his life, we shall better understand the history of his own genius, and of what has seemed to many the decline of it. We shall see that in reality it has not declined at all, and that it is the age that has changed, not he. His own powers still remain what they were. All he has lacked latterly has been adequate use to put them to. We purpose first to consider what these powers are—to consider, that is (if we may again use the simile), what is the material of the mirror before we criticise the reflection.

Poets are divided commonly into two great classes, for which the current antithetic names are *lyrical* and *dramatic*. The division is a true one, and corresponds with a well-known fact; but the names, we think, are both inadequate and confusing. The nature of the difference which they serve so ill to indicate, is we conceive, this. Each class of poet exhibits human nature; but the one does so through the characteristics that individualise men, the other through the characteristics that unite them. The one shows us human characters, the other the human character. Shakespeare is a poet of the first order, Mr. Tennyson of the second. It will be seen that, as a rule, and with but one or two marked exceptions, the characters Mr. Tennyson has treated with most effect are of interest because they are without any private personality. The sentiments and the thoughts are appropriate to the average man or woman, and all that is individual in the case is the material or the mental circumstances. Let us take, for instance, the fine poem of 'Ulysses,' and contrast it with 'The Northern Farmer.' The first of these is typical of Mr. Tennyson's usual treatment; the last is an exception to it. The Northern farmer is a special, an individual character. He is of interest to us because he is strange and external to us. To borrow a phrase from philosophy that is rather plain than elegant, he is emphatically the *not-me*. But with Ulysses the case is exactly opposite. His feelings, his aspirations interest us because, or in so far as, they are a fragment of the *me*.

> I am a part of all that I have met;
> Yet all experience is an arch wherethro'
> Gleams that untravell'd world, whose margin fades
> For ever and for ever when I move.
> How dull it is to pause, to make an end,
> To rust unburnish'd, not to shine in use!
> As tho' to breathe were life. Life piled on life
> Were all too little, and of one to me
> Little remains: but every hour is saved
> From that eternal silence.

All these, it is plain, are not individual thoughts and sentiments. They are what, under the required conditions, are to some extent shared by every man. Let us compare them with those of the Northern farmer. There is a *bizarre* likeness between the two, which will make the difference clearer, as in both cases the thing represented is an active man confronting the approach of death.

> Do godamoighty knaw what a's doing a-taäkin' o' mea?
> I beänt wonn as saws 'ere a beän an' yonder a pea;
> An' Squoire 'ull be sa mad an' all—a' dear a' dear!
> And I'a managed for Squoire coom Michaelmas thutty year.

It will be seen that the idea in the farmer's mind is much the same as that attributed to Ulysses. Both men think it vile

> To rust unburnish'd, not to shine in use.

Both long to save something from 'that eternal silence.' But this longing is specialised in the one case; it is universalised, by symbolism, in the other. Now it is true that, in the case of the 'Northern Farmer,' Mr. Tennyson has specialised with singular success. He has done the same thing also in certain other poems. But if we take his genius and his works as a whole, to do this is not characteristic of him. What he does for the most part is the exact opposite of this; and it is through such opposite treatment that his chief work has been accomplished. It has been said of Hamlet that he is not a man, but that he is man. A similar, though not the same remark, might be made of Mr. Tennyson's chief creations. We can say of nearly all of them that they are not men; we can say of no one of them that he is man; but they are each of them certain parts of man. They represent the general human character, as Mr. Tennyson sees it developed in certain directions, or stirred and sometimes distorted by certain events or passions.

Few students of the Arthurian Idylls can fail to be struck with this. The men and women described in them are no doubt diverse; but they are not, properly speaking, so much diverse characters as diverse characteristics. Arthur, for instance, is virtue; he is not a virtuous man: he is virtue, distilled out of man in general, not embodied in one man in particular. The same may be said of Lancelot; he too is a distillation. He is simply Arthur, with a baser element added. And these two figures are typical. All the men and women of the Idylls are creatures of a like substance, with but one or two exceptions, and these unimportant. Contrast Mr. Tennyson's heroes with those of the Homeric poems, and the fact is at once apparent. Achilles, Hector, and Ulysses—these are men, they are not qualities. They are embodiments; Mr. Tennyson's are disembodiments. In the Homeric poems we see various men and women; in Mr. Tennyson's poems we see self under various conditions; we see self as it may be, or as it might be.

> I am thyself: what hast thou done to me?
> And I, and I, thyself—lo, each one saith.

Nor must the variety of the forms mislead us in which self is thus presented. In all, or in nearly all, there is one of two things—the common male self or the common female self; only they are shown to us under all influences. They are shown us modified by youth and age, by thought, by passion, and by affection, by moral perplexities, and by evil or good volition. But through all these varied circumstances we have still the common character. The remarkable scene in which Vivien ruins Merlin may strike us, at first sight, as dramatic, in the common sense of the word. But it is really not so. The actors in it are really not a man and woman. They are the wise man's weakness and the wicked woman's attraction. Mr. Tennyson, it is true, has attempted to make one of them more than this; but in so far as he has done so, he has failed. He has tried to make his Vivien an individual. He has tried to give her some special personal character. He has given her certain tricks of speech and ways of smiling ' saucily,' and he has doubtless accomplished something in the direction aimed at. But with what result? Vivien as an abstraction is worthy of Mr. Tennyson. Vivien as a special young lady is worthy of Mr. Anthony Trollope. According to the common use of the word *dramatic*, we doubt if Mr.

Tennyson has been dramatic in any memorable way, excepting in the case of 'The Northern Farmer.' Gawain is a spirited sketch; Limours is a delicate one; Sir Kaye the seneschal though slight and coarse, is a distinct one; and there are many more of the same degree of merit. But it is not here that we must look for Mr. Tennyson's true powers. We must look for them, as we have said already, in his revelations of man and woman, not in his creations of separate men and women.

It seems to be accepted as very nearly an axiom, that creative art, such as that of the Homeric poems or of Shakespeare, is, of all forms of art, the highest. We are not concerned to dispute or deny this. We may concede that Mr. Tennyson's art is but art of the second order; but it has certain qualities of its own that belong to no other kind. It may not do all that creative art *can* do, but it does certain things that creative art can *not* do; and it is suited in a special manner to the age that Mr. Tennyson has been born in. It is on this point that we now desire to dwell.

Mr. Tennyson's age is in many ways peculiar. We have contrasted his art already with that of

H

Shakespeare. We may contrast his age with that of Shakespeare also. In both, life and thought have been exceptionally active; but the activity has taken very different forms, and has been the result of very different forces. In the first, it was the activity of action. In the second, it has been the activity of reflection. For Shakespeare the question was, what shall men do? For Mr. Tennyson it has been, what shall man do? Life, as Shakespeare knew it, was intenser in some ways than it has ever been since; and thought, in some ways, was as active then as now. But thought was quickened without being bewildered; and scepticism was not afraid of itself from suspecting, in any degree, its own ultimate tendencies. As to theology, it is true, the human mind was in a ferment; but scepticism as to theologies was but a sign of faith in theology. The infinite solemnity of every human life, the infinite importance of each separate human destiny—these were things that were not questioned or doubted of. As to thought and feeling on practical moral questions, the ethics of Catholic Christendom were still dominant. The Catholic ideal was still the unquestioned standard. What is noble in man and what is pure in woman—all men were agreed on these points ; and as to the value as well as to the nature of virtue their consent was equally unanimous. The extraordinary power of the great Elizabethan drama is mainly due to this. Every action in life, to the thought of that age, was either a triumph or a catastrophe ; and the strongest evidence of this fact is, in many places, the poet's silence about it. What we never doubt of, we have no need to affirm. Mr. Ruskin has divided poets into two classes, one of which, he says, has the ascending vision, the other the descending. Thus Dante looked upwards to heaven, Shakespeare downwards to earth. And this may be true enough. But though Shakespeare may only have seen the earth, he saw it by the light of heaven ; and the same is true, too, of his fellow-poets and his epoch.

But now all is changed. What in Shakespeare's days men took for granted, in Mr. Tennyson's they have had to fight for, to question, and to reconsider. They have had to seek for the site of their city, not to make designs for their houses. Human nature, as Mr. Tennyson has found it, is at a singular crisis in its history. When he first began to look about him, 'ideas,' as George Eliot says, 'with fresh vigour were making armies of themselves.' New scientific knowledge, new political aspirations were forcing themselves into the common consciousness, and the old elements with the new were forming unfamiliar combinations. The world was waking up to the condition that for three centuries it had been preparing for itself, and it was waking up to it with hope, and fear, and wonder. It was in such a state that Mr. Tennyson found it—a state unparalleled in any preceding age; and this fact is reflected in all his works. He found the common circumstances by which the men of his time were united more important than their private and personal varieties. They differed more from the men of other ages than they did from each other; or this common difference was, at all events, of a more pressing and profound significance. Human souls might each have their own vicissitudes; but the human soul was undergoing one more important. The spiritual climate was rapidly changing round it, and it had to adapt itself to new fashions of life. How should this be done? That was the great question. What was the extent, and what the nature, of the change? How much of the old could man retain? How should this much be reconciled with what was strange and new? The issue was one of infinite complexity. Most men could but discern some fragment of it. Mr. Tennyson has discerned, we do not say the whole, but more of it certainly than any of his English contemporaries. He may not on any subject possess the knowledge of a specialist; but he has grasped with astonishing accuracy the salient points—the points of common moment—in countless branches of thought and of discovery, and he has seen their bearing on the daily life of man.

How accurate this grasp has been, we may illustrate by a single example—the example of the short poem of 'Lucretius.' The beauties of this masterpiece have met with but little recognition generally; and from the very nature of the subject it must necessarily be obscure to many. Its poetic qualities, however, we are now not concerned to insist upon; what we refer to is the intellectual power displayed in it. The Lucretian philosophy is in places very obscure, and it has been beyond the power of many of the most accomplished scholars to expound clearly some of the author's scientific conceptions. But

Mr. Tennyson, in his short poem, has done more than a score of commentators. On the dark places of the 'De rerum naturâ' his verses fall like a beam of sunlight. He conveys more in a line than others have done in chapters. Never, for instance, has the aim of the Roman poet been interpreted so vividly as in the following passage, where Mr. Tennyson makes him speak of

> My golden work in which I told a truth
> That stays the rolling Ixionian wheel,
> And numbs the Fury's ringlet-snake, and plucks
> The mortal soul from out immortal hell.

But an example can be given more striking even than this. Of all the obscure parts of the system of Lucretius, the most obscure is perhaps his theory of vision. It is a difficult thing to understand clearly: it is still more difficult to express clearly. Any student who has tried to master this matter, and comes fresh upon Mr. Tennyson's allusions to it, can hardly fail to be startled by the sudden illumination they afford him. Lucretius is made to describe his impure dreams as

> The phantom husks of something foully done,
> And fleeting through the boundless universe.

And in another moment he goes on thus to question himself:—

> How should the mind, except it loved them, clasp
> These idols to herself? or do they fly
> Now thinner, and now thicker, like the flakes
> In a fall of snow, and so press in, perforce
> Of multitude, as crowds that in an hour
> Of civic tumult jam the doors, and bear
> The keepers down, and throng, their rags and they
> The basest, far into that council-hall
> Where sit the best and stateliest of the land?

In these passages, more especially in the single line—

> The phantom husks of something foully done—

there is a grasp displayed of an extremely intricate subject, and a magical power of making an obscure subject lucid, to which in any writer it would be hard to find a parallel. And as Mr. Tennyson has mastered ancient thought, so in the same way has he mastered modern. And herein lies one of the chief secrets of his influence. He has had a broad intellectual grasp of those unique and diverse circumstances that have given its character to our age.

The poet, however, needs more than such powers of intellect; and Mr. Tennyson possesses more. We have said that what he deals with is the common human character, and he understands and he treats this like a master. We may describe him as busy with two distinct heroes—the Spirit of the Age, and the Spirit of Human Nature; and his theme is the latter of these as making terms with the former. Human nature in its broadest and most general sense—of this he has a consummate knowledge. He knows its good and evil, and all its various workings, whether glad or sad, tender or terrible. He knows the qualities in it that are of all time, as well as the circumstances of it that are of his own time. Such knowledge, on its more philosophic side, he manifested very early. There are three poems of his, all written before he was twenty-six, which most men have to live ten years longer before they can understand properly. We refer to 'The Palace of Art,' 'The Vision of Sin,' and the short stanzas called 'Will.' All these show a piercing vision, a prophetic vision also, of the needs of the human soul, and the result on it of certain courses. The young man writes with all the wisdom of the old; and in the first two of the three poems named the wisdom is all the more remarkable, because the language it is expressed in is sometimes almost puerile in its freshness. As an artistic production the 'Palace of Art' is poor; so is the 'Vision of Sin' also. In neither is the style sufficiently chastened. The poet, with a boy's glee, has introduced boyish ornament. But the matter is in startling contrast. What he deals with is no youthful feeling, but the barren years that succeed to a youth misspent. The real burden of his story is the sorrows of the soul in middle and in old age, and these are described with all the prescient force of genius. The bitterness and the lonely cynicism that are the doom of vice and selfishness are not realised by most men till the time has come to feel them; but Mr. Tennyson knew or foreknew them when he was yet in the dawn of manhood. At the very time when he could describe the purest and the most trusting love—the love of a young man—with all a young man's sympathy, he could describe the blighted soul, in this way, also :—

> Deep dread and loathing of her solitude
> Fell on her, from which mood was born
> Scorn of herself; again, from out that mood
> Laughter at her self-scorn.

. . . . . .

> But in dark corners of her palace stood
>   Uncertain shapes; and unawares
> On white-eyed phantasms weeping tears of blood,
>   And horrible nightmares,
>
> And hollow shades enclosing hearts of flame,
>   And, with dim fretted foreheads all,
> On corpses three-months-old at noon she came,
>   That stood against the wall.

In all this there is an almost ghastly vividness, and of the 'Vision of Sin' we may say the same thing, whilst in the poem of 'Will' the well-known concluding stanza has all the precision of a profound philosophic statement, and all the passionate despair of a soul that has proved the tragic truth of it.

> He seems as one whose footsteps halt,
> Toiling in immeasurable sand,
> And o'er a weary sultry land,
> Far beneath a blazing vault,
> Sown in a wrinkle of the monstrous hill,
> The city sparkles like a grain of salt.

Seeing Mr. Tennyson thus a master of the more complex problems of life, and those presumably most remote from his own experience, it is small wonder that he was master of things more near to him. Instances will occur to all, so readily that we need not cite them, of his early command of the universal passions—of maternal, of sexual, and of divine love; of the desire for rest and the desire for action; of hope and of sorrow. Such poems as 'Locksley Hall,' 'The May Queen,' and 'The Lotos-Eaters' have, for this reason, become household words. As he has lived on, the same power has become matured, and we can pronounce him, as we know him now, one of the greatest masters of pathos to be found in any age. His command, in short, is over all those emotions and situations which impart their own interest to the persons concerned with them, and do not derive it from them. Within such limits he has few rivals.

These qualifications, however, would have been but of small avail, had it not been for one other. We have spoken already of his matter. What we speak of now is his form. It may be doubted if any poet since the days of Horace and Virgil has been so great a master of the mere art of expression; and there is more in this than there may at first sight seem to be. It may be thought that expression is a mere affair of words; but it is not so. We include in expression not only the words which convey the meaning directly, but the scenic surroundings, the remote allusions, and the side touches that accompany it, and by which the mind and the imagination are prepared and tuned for its reception. Such art is one of the last refinements, one of the last luxuries of poetry; and it is not characteristic of the poets of the greatest ages. It is proper to poets who have had to sing under difficulties, and who, to collect listeners, are obliged first to fascinate them. The interest in Homer lies mainly in what he says; in Horace, in Virgil, and in Mr. Tennyson, it lies equally in how they say it. The relation of the thought to the expression charms us, as well as the relation of the thought to ourselves: it is possible, indeed, that the latter may be quite trivial, and yet the former give us great pleasure. Mr. Tennyson's earlier verses will afford us many examples of this. Here, for instance, are some stanzas, which, though sufficiently slight in meaning, have two phrases in them as felicitous as any of Horace :—

> Go fetch a pint of port:
> But let it not be such as that
> You set before chance-comers,
> *But such whose father-grape grew fat*
> *On Lusitanian summers.*

And in the same poem the poet speaks of a vintage which

> Stow'd, when classic Canning died,
>   In musty bins and chambers,
> *Had cast upon its crusted side*
>   *The gloom of ten Decembers.*

The 'Lyrical Monologue,' from which these lines are quoted, is nothing but a plaything, and not, as a whole, a pretty one. But the nature and the perfection of skill is sometimes best illustrated by the waste of it. Here is another example of the poet's manner, on which we shall dwell somewhat more at length.

> Come down, O maid, from yonder mountain height :
> What pleasure lives in height (the shepherd sang),
> In height and cold, the splendour of the hills ?
> But cease to move so near the heavens, and cease
> To glide a sunbeam by the blasted pine,
> To sit a star upon the sparkling spire ;
> And come, for Love is of the valley, come,
> For Love is of the valley, come thou down
> And find him ; by the happy threshold, he,
> Or hand in hand with Plenty in the maize,
> Or red with spirted purple of the vats,
> Or foxlike in the vine ; nor cares to walk
> With Death and Morning on the silver horns,
> Nor wilt thou snare him in the white ravine,
> Nor find him dropt upon the firths of ice,

>   That huddling slant in furrow-cloven falls
>   To roll the torrent out of dusky doors :
>   But follow. Let the torrent dance thee down
>   To find him in the valley ; let the wild
>   Lean-headed eagles yelp alone, and leave
>   The monstrous ledges there to slope and spill
>   Their thousand wreaths of dangling water-smoke,
>   That like a broken purpose waste in air.
>   So waste not thou : but come ; for all the vales
>   Await thee : azure pillars of the hearth
>   Arise to thee; the children call, and I
>   Thy shepherd pipe, and sweet is every sound,
>   Sweeter thy voice, but every sound is sweet ;
>   Myriads of rivulets hurrying through the lawn,
>   The moan of doves in immemorial elms,
>   And murmuring of innumerable bees.

We have quoted this passage because in its short compass there are illustrations of all Mr. Tennyson's chief technical excellences. The actual meaning, the actual thought, is simple. There is nothing in it very striking or passionate ; but as an example of expression it is wonderful. The thought is buoyed up, is prolonged and amplified, as a single clause of a prayer is by an elaborate piece of music. Other thoughts and remote images, are summoned from all quarters to throw light upon it, and to make our own feelings resonant as it touches them. Phrases and epithets are used with an astonish ing precision. Flying ideas and pictures are snared by them, as though by a hunter's lasso.

> Let the wild
> Lean-headed eagles yelp alone, and leave
> The monstrous ledges there to slope and spill
> Their thousand wreaths of dangling water-smoke.

In these lines we have a landscape like one of Turner's. Every word in it is a study. Here, again, the verse has a different quality.

> Nor cares to walk
> With Death and Morning on the silver horns.

This single touch reminds one of Milton by the magical stimulus that it gives to the imagination. It produces a feeling in us as though our thoughts were being caught away by a wind. And all these powers are here employed by the poet to convey a thought or a sentiment which is in itself a commonplace. Love is a domestic, not a transcendental passion: that is the long and short of the whole of it. As related to ourselves, this may not have much interest; but as related to the way in which Mr. Tennyson has chosen to tell it us, it must enchant and startle every lover of poetry.

The workmanship in the above passages is notably more precious than the material; and we have purposely chosen them, for that reason, as examples of Mr. Tennyson's manner. But that is not because we think that such is the case with him generally. On the contrary, we hold that, in the work that is most distinctive of him, the thought is as profound as the manner is fine and perfect. What we have wished to illustrate has been this. Let thought with Mr. Tennyson be either profound or shallow, he has always, in expressing it, two aims present. One is to express the thought; the other is to connect with the expression some added literary pleasure. He is perpetually offering his audience a large bribe to listen to him. It is to his astonishing skill in this way that much of his success is due. Sometimes, indeed, the skill overreaches its own object. He refines his verbal workmanship to the verge of weakness, and his allusion and imagery sometimes produce obscurity. But take him for all in all, he ranks the first of English poets in making the act of expression a luxury and a perfect ornament.

To sum up, then, what we have thus far observed about him, his chief characteristics amount to these. In the first place, he is a man of wide intellectual grasp. He has understood his age, and its various complex tendencies, like a divine, a philosopher, a politician and a physicist. He understands, in the second place, the common human character, and is a complete master of its more universal manifestations. He has studied this character with special reference to the conditions now surrounding it. And he has finally an unrivalled gift for expressing his own meaning, and for compelling others to attend to it. Thus, in studying his works, let us be clear what we can look to find in them. We are not to look there for complex dramatic action, nor even for the unfolding of any great and sustained story. Small stories he tells well and skilfully ; but to these his power is limited. The Arthurian Idylls, as a whole, it is true, suggest a story, but they suggest it only, they do not tell it. They are stars in a constellation, and the astronomer fills the figure in. They but approach an epic near enough to make us feel how far they are from it. Nor are we to expect from him, on the other hand, any birdlike lyrical outbursts. The true lyrist presents us with one special man—himself. The true dramatist presents us with many men. Mr. Tennyson does neither. He presents us with the

I

common self—common to him and all of us; he presents us with such of its workings and vicissitudes as we might conceivably all experience; and he presents us with it in special connection with the conditions of the present century.

And now let us examine a little more closely from what standpoint he does this. His position we think, at least to a late period, can be defined with sufficient clearness. He may be said to represent and to have helped largely to formulate the scientific optimism of the early Victorian epoch. That optimism then was not what it is now. In the world of thought events have been moving rapidly. The last few decades have done the work of centuries, and it needs an effort to realise how matters stood but forty, thirty, or even twenty years ago. This, however, we must try to do, if we would understand Mr. Tennyson's history. The facts of the case are simple, and can be stated briefly. Mr. Tennyson's development has coincided with two great events—the growth in England of the modern democratic principle, and the general diffusion of modern religious scepticism—and with both of these events his career is closely associated. The earliest poems of his which he has thought worth preserving appeared a few months after the passing of the first Reform Bill, and must have been composed during the times of popular agitation that preceded it. A year later, at a cost of twenty millions, slavery was abolished in all the British colonies, and for the first time it could be said that our rule was over none but freemen. Two years later was seen the birth of a national education system, and the passing of a new Poor Law. The people at large were finding their voice on all sides, and in many quarters began to use it with violence. Demands were made presently for further parliamentary reforms, and the political privileges of property were attacked openly, and not without success. At the same time there was formed an Anti-Corn-Law League and the gospel of free trade was preached with a religious enthusiasm. In seven years' time the preaching bore its fruit. The Corn Laws were repealed in 1846, and the Free-trade policy under Lord John Russell was carried at once into every branch of commerce. Six years afterwards came the great industrial exhibition, which contained contributions from nearly every nation. This was a huge material symbol of a new form of optimism and at the same time a stimulus to it. Popular sympathy and imagination began to take a wider flight, and visions filled the air of a universal human brotherhood. Wars were to cease; there was to be a millennium of trade and of benevolence. Events, however, soon convinced the most sanguine that such a consummation was to be, at any rate, not immediate. But a year or two passed, and England was at war with Russia, and the spirit of militant patriotism dealt somewhat roughly with the mild enthusiasm of humanity.

The events we have thus briefly glanced at cover a period of some twenty-five years, and it is of that period in especial that Mr. Tennyson is the interpreter. Its ideas have been the ideas of his heart, and its hopes have been the hopes of his heart. We have touched as yet on its political aspect only. Its religious aspect is no less remarkable. During that quarter of a century science and scientific scepticism, for the first time in England, began to be widely popular and to leaven thought at large. For the first time the general lay mind began to examine critically the great teachings of Revelation, to confront them with those of science, and to be startled at the two as they were placed together. Men who lament the fact, and men who rejoice over it, are to be heard now on all sides proclaiming the spread of infidelity; but at the time we speak of, though so little removed from ours, the national faith was strong. Men were not then prepared for even such moderate exhibitions of free-thought as 'Ecce Homo' or the volume of 'Essays and Reviews.' They still felt secure in their old traditional position, and conceived that the modern view of the Cosmos could be harmonised easily with their own. In the religious world for a time this produced a strange activity, tinged with the same facile optimism that was to be discerned in politics, and very closely connected with it. Not only were all peoples to be united, but all creeds were to be united also. Some looked forward to a union of all the sacerdotal churches, others to the advent of some simpler form of Christianity. But various as such hopes may have been in detail, they had all one common quality—they were all Christian, and they all pointed to progress.

Such was the picture on its sunny side, but it had its dark side as well. In the world of thought, though as yet they worked in secret, the spirits of denial and of materialism were already active. Deism was dead and done with. What the Christian had now to meet was Atheism. And in social life as well this creed had its counterpart. It was all very good that the world should 'fill with commerce,' and magic argosies be laden 'with costly bales;' but the cultus of trade and industry, as it was then practically adopted, looked under certain aspects like the most sordid and heathen Mammon-worship. The august and inspiring spectacle of universal progress was in danger of changing itself into that of a struggle for base luxury. None of these facts were lost upon Mr. Tennyson. He knew his generation both in its good and evil; but he believed the good principle to be the stronger of the two, and he tried to show his generation where its own strength lay.

To this end he has dwelt throughout all his works on certain modes of life and on certain moral qualities. He has tried to exhibit by every means in his power their beauty and their sanctity; he has contrasted them with their opposites, and he has done all he could to harmonise them with their present environment. These modes of life and these qualities are not many in number. They amount, we think, to these—love, friendship, domesticity, patriotism, cosmopolitanism, and undogmatic Christianity. He has presented them to us under every conceivable form, and connected with every conceivable circumstance, and he has used all his matchless skill to bring home to his audience their beauty or their intellectual fitness. He tries so to show them to us that we may believe from seeing them.

Such is his constant method when he deals with love. The passion of the lover for him is but the sunrise of the affections of the husband, and he has consistently striven to connect it as such with every thought of mental and emotional satisfaction, and every image of spiritual and physical beauty. He has linked and interfused it with all the fairest aspects of nature—with sunset and with sunrise, with flowers, with meadows, and a thousand homely scenes, and he has done this generally with an art that conceals itself. The picture and the passion he puts side by side, and the two coalesce spontaneously. 'Maud,' which, in our judgment, is one of the finest love-poems in our language, is full of this quality. There are also exquisite instances of it in his earlier idylls. The following passage is from one of these last. 'Should my shadow,' says the lover to his beloved—he is parted for ever from her, not by faults, but by misfortune —'should my shadow cross thy dreams'—

> Oh might it come like one that looks content,
> With quiet eyes unfaithful to the truth,
> And point thee forward to a distant light,
> Or seem to lift a burden from thy heart
> And leave thee freer, till thou wake refreshed
> Then when the first low matin-chirp hath grown
> Full quire, and morning driven her plow of pearl
> Far furrowing into light the mounded rack,
> Beyond the fair green field and eastern sea.

In the same way, whenever he treats this passion, he is constantly mixing it with some sight or sound of beauty. And these sights and sounds are no vague abstractions. They are things that we are all of us familiar with; they are the common things of our own English life. Mr. Tennyson's love has nothing transcendental about it. Its home is the earth, and not the air; and here lies the secret of its power.

It purifies earth because it does not disdain to inhabit it.

> Am I not the nobler through thy love?
> Oh three times less unworthy! likewise thou
> Art more through love.

Mr. Tennyson's whole philosophy of the subject is comprised in these lines. In a certain sense the philosophy is not peculiar to him, but in a certain sense it is. Though the passion of love is as old as human nature itself, yet in different ages it has assumed special aspects, and taken special places in man's moral view of life. This is markedly true of the present century, and true still more of those years of it which at present we have in view. The progressive and hopeful school of religious thinkers, all, during that period, took one direction. The more rigid forms of orthodoxy, they began to think, were untenable. These, all of them, were associated with the ascetic view of life; and our highest duty with regard to human affection was according to them little more than curbing it. What the progressive school aimed at was to reverse this condition of things. In proportion as they thought it hopeless to formulate what was divine, they sought to deify what was human.

They preached a new gospel: we were not to check our nature, but to develop it. The delights of affection which had all along been permitted man were no longer presented as concessions to our weakness, but as the chief elements of our strength. The allowed indulgence became the enjoined duty. We were no longer to prevent love running away with us; we were to make it run away with us till it brought us to the gates of heaven.

It is this view of the matter that Mr. Tennyson has assimilated, and of which he is the most perfect and the most influential spokesman. Here at least, he teaches us, we have one thing stable, one thing beyond the reach of scepticism, and a nucleus and a rallying-point for all that is valuable in life. Sensuous beauty adorns and is hallowed by it; material refinements are chastened and spiritualised by it; and the true meaning of Christianity is unlocked by it. Mr. Tennyson is the prophet *par excellence*, of affection thus regarded; and his two longest and most important works are a deliberate exposition of its nature and its varied influence. The two works we allude to are 'In Memoriam' and 'The Arthurian Idylls.' The subject of both is the same; only it is treated under different aspects.

'In Memoriam' deals with love as connected with faith; the 'Idylls' deal with it as connected with practice.

The former of these is in many ways unique. In no other poem that we know of is there so complete a fusion of profound thought and passion. We have an intense feeling presented to us as related to its proximate cause, and also as adjusting itself to the deepest claims of philosophy. At one and the same time it is both expressed and vindicated. Every theory of physical and social evolution, every latest speculation as to the nature of life and its immortality, mixes in the mind of the poet over the grave of his dead friend; and he disarms of its terrors every seemingly hostile doctrine, or else discovers in it food for faith and comfort. The mastery which he displays over both branches of his subject is no less astonishing than the way in which he unites the two. Not only does his science penetrate his passion, and his passion breathe a living soul into his science, but the latter is as comprehensive and accurate as the former is deep and tender. Every one of his illustrations, as it were, is a picture by a great master, and every picture is a scientific diagram. In the following two stanzas there is a geological treatise epitomised; but the events dealt with are not so much chronicled as exhibited.

> There rolls the deep, where grew the tree.
>   Oh earth, what changes hast thou seen!
>   There where the long street roars hath been
> The stillness of the central sea.
>
> The hills are shadows, and they flow
>   From form to form, and nothing stands;
>   They melt like mist, the solid lands,
> Like clouds they shape themselves and go.

And then in another instant the poet proceed thus:—

> But in my spirit will I dwell,
>   And dream my dream, and hold it true;
>   For tho' my lips may breathe adieu,
> I cannot think the thing farewell.
>
> . . . . .
>
> If e'er when faith had fall'n asleep,
>   I heard a voice 'believe no more'
>   And heard an ever-breaking shore
> That tumbled in the Godless deep;
>
> A warmth within the breast would melt
>   The freezing reason's colder part,
>   And like a man in wrath the heart
> Stood up and answer'd 'I have felt.'
>
> . . . . .
>
> And what I am beheld again
>   What is, and no man understands;
>   And out of darkness came the hands
> That reach through nature, moulding men.'

Such is the soul's attitude, with regard to physical science on the one hand and to religion on the other, which Mr. Tennyson in 'In Memoriam' reveals to his generation. The lines just quoted form a key to the whole poem. The poem in many ways is full of change and variety; but the poet through all this does but alternate between two subjects—love as a passion that is experienced, and love as a mystery that is to be expounded. 'In Memoriam' stands alone for the way in which these are dealt with. It is in form but the personal expression of one man's regret for another. In reality it is a revelation to an age of its own struggle after some new spiritual stand-point.

So, too, with the Idylls, the real hero through all of them is not this knight or that knight; the hero is pure human affection : only affection here is presented not as the germ of faith, but as the source of beneficent conduct. As in 'In Memoriam' it is treated as purifying and giving vision to the soul, so in the Idylls it is exhibited as inspiring and ennobling life, and as being not only the germ of faith, but the motive power in all social progress. Of all Mr. Tennyson's works, the Idylls, or at least the four earlier

ones, have been the most widely popular; bu[t]
we doubt if they will be the most enduring[.]
The period and the life they deal with are no[t]
only too remote from our own, but they are
poorly fitted to represent, even symbolically, the
duties and the aspirations of to-day. To figh[t]
the heathen, and to put down brigandage, is bu[t]
a meagre symbol of complex modern activity[.]
A tournament hardly seems to us a test of [a]
man's most valuable or most interesting quali[-]
ties; and a serious reader can hardly fail to b[e]
wearied by the perpetual recurrence of singl[e]
combats the unhorsing of horsemen, the splin[-]
tering of lances, and the cleaving of helmets[.]
Had Mr. Tennyson's power been more dramatic
this would have mattered less. Through the
sameness of such incidents we should have dis[-]
cerned various personalities, with their specia[l]
hopes and aims; and these might have give[n]
the incidents their own variety and significance[.]
But Mr. Tennyson is not dramatic. If we com[-]
pare his poetry with the prose romances it i[s]
founded on, we shall realise this more clearl[y]
than ever. In the prose romances nearly ever[y]
character is a complete man or woman, with [a]
complete human individuality. This individ[u-]

ality Mr. Tennyson has not only in no way developed, he has not even retained it in its distinctness. On the contrary, he would seem to have done his utmost not to develop but to obliterate it. And thus the result is that on which we have already commented. We have qualities and situations; we have not men and women. Such being the case, we again repeat our judgment that though certain qualities of human nature are developed with extreme power in the Idylls, the situations, as a rule, are for the most part insufficient, and are often not far from puerile. The environment of the organism, if we may so speak, does not represent adequately the environment of modern man. And yet this is evidently what the case requires it should do. Mr. Tennyson, in his study of human nature, is essentially not an antiquarian. If it is not modern man that he studies, he studies nothing. His Idylls are no contributions to the spiritual history of the past; they are meant to be pictures of the spiritual condition of the present. Every thought and every sentiment of his knights and ladies is essentially of our own century; it is in that fact that their interest lies: and it is for this reason we regret the limits of the stage on which he has chosen to exhibit them.

In spite, however, of this fundamental want, the Idylls doubtless fulfil much of their writer's intention, and exhibit many of his very finest qualities. Taken together as one connected poem, it is true they lack unity. They form but the hints of a great design which the artist has not had strength to execute. They are merely so many stepping-stones for our own constructive imagination. But, taken separately, they are true works of art. The story in each is unfolded with grace and skill, and that power of expression on which we have dwelt already is conspicuous everywhere. It is not, however, on these points that we are concerned to dwell now. What we wish to note is, that, in spite of much that is wanting, the Arthurian Idylls are, within certain limits, a representation of a modern fact. They represent the modern religious spirit, springing from the human heart, and fusing itself with historical Christianity; and they represent it, imperfectly it is true, but still distinctly, as taking science by the hand, and with its aid setting to reform the world.

In this connection we must notice another poem, 'Aylmer's Field.' Human affection is again the central theme. The characters in the story are treated according to the usual method. Their situations make them, not they the situations. It is enough for the poet's purpose that they are human beings. All he desires to show is the passions and the influences that act through them, and what he deals with in this case is the dark and not the bright side of progress. He deals with love as thwarted by the demands of an artificial civilisation, and as crying out from its grave against the forces that have destroyed it.

Of these three works we have been dwelling on, 'In Memoriam,' the Arthurian Idylls, and the short tale just mentioned, the first was published in 1850, the four finest of the second in 1859, and the third in 1864. The first only belongs, so far as time goes, to that quarter of a century which we conceive in especial to be Mr. Tennyson's own; but the others, though not given to the world within its limits, are yet equally its spiritual children, and are the result of its temper and its philosophies. In the same set of works are of course included also the two early volumes, 'The Princess' and 'Maud;' and these, taken together, comprise the fullest results of Mr. Tennyson's genius. We must now repeat what we said at starting. The above results are the fullest, not because Mr. Tennyson's genius has since declined, but because the materials his age has supplied him with have since changed in quality. That special period which we have called his own was one of the most exciting periods to be anywhere found in history. It saw the blossoming, if not the bud, of half the wonders of the century, and to an English eye especially, it was full of splendid promise. Distress and poverty, it is true, were not wanting; but year by year their voice was heard, and year by year some abuse was remedied. Freedom in England seemed growing visibly, and, contrasted with Continental troubles, peace seemed growing also. It was this period that was ushered in not only with the first Reform Bill, but with the first railroads; and commerce developed itself even more rapidly than freedom. Science, as we have already said, had freed religion from her trammels without depriving her of her supports. All human life was then in eager movement. A new world had been discovered in the very midst of the old. Progress, and rapid progress, towards some ever-bettering state seemed a matter at that time not of faith only, but of sight.

> Bliss was it in that dawn
> To live, but to be young was very heaven.

That was said of the times of the first French Revolution. It may be said with equal truth of the earlier times of Queen Victoria. For the earnest and the courageous that was the age of confident optimism, and of this Mr. Tennyson, in poetry, has been the great national exponent. It is this that he has made his own; it was on this that he staked his hopes; it was by the spirit of this optimism that his poetic character was fashioned. But the years of promise went by, and they were not succeeded by any years of performance—or, at least, there was no performance adequate to the hopes of the sanguine. We say this with a reservation. To the sanguine of a certain class there was indeed performance, but those were not men with the faiths of Mr. Tennyson. They were the extreme apostles of atheism and revolution, whereas Mr. Tennyson was conservative even in his liberalism, and was, above all, profoundly religious. It is hard to believe, therefore, that the world, as for the last twenty years he has looked on it, has not in many ways been growing a darker sight to him. His faith in progress may be still firm, but the fact of it has not been visible to him. It is true that in his own creed he has provided against such a trial. It is part of the teaching of his Idylls, taken collectively, that apparent failure is not final failure, and that advance is not to be doubted of because of tragic relapses. And it may well be that, even during these latter years, he can catch, as clearly as ever—

> A deeper voice across the storm,
> Proclaiming social truth shall spread,
>   And justice, even though thrice again
>   The red fool-fury of the Seine
> Should pile her barricades with dead.

But though his intellectual faith may assure him of the truth of this, it can hardly be doubted that sight, so far as the present goes, has told him a different tale. Social truth and justice have not spread as rapidly as he once dreamed they would, and there is another side of progress which must have disappointed him still more. We mean the progress, or, at least, the change in the relationship between religion and science. We see signs to us very plain, in Mr. Tennyson's later poems, that the course of thought upon these subjects has profoundly affected him, and that, though it has not weakened his faith, it has given a sombre tone to it. His first literary expression of this is to be found, we think, in 'Lucretius,' which was published in 1868. That poem seems significant of two facts—the hostile fascination for him of the doctrines of scientific materialism, and the desolate deductions that, if true, it suggested to him. Despite the historical accuracy with which he treats his subject, there is something of the modern world that he breathes through the life of the Roman—the modern world as he was beginning to re-conceive it.

> I often grew
> Tired of so much within our little life,
> Or of so little in our little life—
> Poor little life that toddles half an hour
> Crowned with a flower or two, and there an end.

That Mr. Tennyson would avow these as his own sentiments, we do not for a moment say. But we do say that they are the sentiments the age was suggesting to him, and that his artistic mirror now reflected gloom, where, fifteen years before, it had been reflecting brightness.

There are further facts which support us in this opinion. After the publication of 'Lucretius' Mr. Tennyson's next feat was the completion of the Arthurian Idylls; and this done, he betook himself to a new form of poetry—the historic drama. In 1875 he published 'Queen Mary,' and, two years later, 'Harold.' Now these dramas display many masterly qualities. Being the work of Mr. Tennyson, it would be strange if they did not. But there is one thing wanting in them, and that is inspiration. We feel all through that the poet is amusing himself; he is not expressing himself. He is delighted in the exercise of his own skill, but his heart is not in the subjects on which his skill is being exercised. Shakespeare's histories spoke at once to the sympathies of his audience: the events and sentiments presented to them were to them living things. They could 'piece out with their thoughts' all artistic imperfections, and their imagination would throng the stage with

> Those very casques
> That did affright the air at Agincourt.

But Mr. Tennyson's dramas make no such appeal

as this to the present London public. 'Harold' is as simply antiquarian as Mr. Freeman's 'History of the Norman Conquest,' nor is anti-Catholic feeling at this day strong enough to give even the interest of hate to a picture of 'bloody Queen Mary.' Mr. Tennyson in composing these dramas, seems to us to have gone into a spiritual retirement, rather than to have kept the spiritual field; and the same may be said also with regard to 'The Cup' and to 'The Falcon.' There is much in each of them to excite literary admiration and even literary criticism. Were we aiming at that, we might dwell longer upon them. But our aim at present lies in another direction. It is not to appraise the value of Mr. Tennyson's separate works in themselves, but to point out the relation of those works to their author, and the relation of their author to his age.

On these points, as we have said before, his last small volume throws an important light; and it is this volume that it now remains for us to consider. Much of its contents we may quietly put aside, not because there is little to praise in them, but because the praise may be taken for granted. We purpose to note only those poems that throw light on Mr. Tennyson's history, and these we take to be the following—' The First Quarrel,' ' The Northern Cobbler,' ' The Village Wife,' and above all, ' Rizpah ' and ' De Profundis.' The first four form a group together, the last stands by itself. We will treat each division separately. The first four poems are all sufficiently remarkable, and convince us of one fact. Mr. Tennyson's command over our common human nature is still as great as ever, and his sympathy with it still as keen and fresh. The ' First Quarrel,' the ' Northern Cobbler,' and the ' Village Wife,' are all in his best manner; whilst of ' Rizpah ' we must say far more than this.

This poem is the story of a poor dying woman, whom an intense shock and sorrow had reduced to madness, and she is represented as telling it to a lady who had come to visit her. Her son, a young man of fine spirit and promise, had fallen among bad companions, and through their influence his manliest characteristic had ruined him.

He lived with a lot of wild mates, and they would not let him be good;
They swore that he dare not rob the mail, and he swore that he would;

And he took no life, but he took one purse, and when all
    was done
He flung it among his fellows—'I'll none of it,' said my son.
I came into court to the judge and the lawyers—I told them
    my tale,
God's own truth—but they kill'd him, they kill'd him for
    robbing the mail.

    .   .   .   .   .   .

Then, since I couldn't but hear that cry of my boy that
    was dead,
They seized me and shut me up; they fastened me down on
    my bed.
'Mother, O mother!'—he called in the dark to me year
    after year—
They beat me for that, they beat me—you know that I
    couldn't but hear;
And then at the last they found I had grown so stupid and
    still,
They let me abroad again; but the creatures had worked
    their will.

What followed was this: Her boy had been hanged in chains, and by the time she was set free again he was nothing but a dangling skeleton, that was falling bone by bone to the ground. When there was no moon, and when the nights were dark, she stole unobserved to the gallows, and night by night collecting what had fallen, she at last laid all of her son that was left her in holy ground.

> Do you think I was scared by the bones? I kissed 'em, I buried 'em all—
> I can't dig deep, I am old—in the night by the churchyard wall.

Such is the outline of the story ; such is the motive of the poem. We feel almost bound to apologise for quoting from it. A work of this character can never be done justice to by quotations. But we have used the above lines with no further end than to indicate baldly the outline of the poet's subject. For his sublime treatment of it, for the tenderness and the terror of his pathos, we must refer the reader to the entire poem itself. Nothing in 'Maud,' nothing in 'Guinevere,' can approach in power to 'Rizpah.'

This fact can, we conceive, be accounted for by the special nature of the subject. Of all human affections, that least subject to change, either in the way of contraction or development, is the passion of mother for child. It asks least aid either from faith or reason. And something similar may be said of the other three poems that we have associated with 'Rizpah.' These three deal all of them with the life of the common people, and touch on feelings and principles in their rudest and simplest form. They take us below the reach of either conscious faith or philosophy; and they elude, they do not meet, the problems of human destiny. Thus Mr. Tennyson's genius has escaped, in these cases, from the external circumstances that had been depressing it; and once supplied with a fitting theme to handle, it has shown itself as strong, if not stronger than ever.

But when we come to the poem called 'De Profundis,' we find it exerting itself under quite other conditions. Just as in the foregoing poems the spirit of the age had been eluded by him, so in this last is it met face to face. Mr. Tennyson here set himself in the year 1880 to repeat what he did exactly thirty years before. He resumed the same task which he had undertaken in 'In Memoriam.' When 'De Profundis' appeared in 'The Nineteenth Century,' it was treated by the weekly journals as some obscure vagary of genius, which might be pardoned, but could certainly not be praised. A more foolish judgment than this we cannot well imagine. The poem is short, but it is, despite its shortness, one of the most significant of all the later works of the author; and, taken in connection with certain parts of 'In Memoriam,' it throws a singular light on his intellectual history. It shows how more and more, as he has lived through the age of science, the multiplying facts of scientific materialism have been pressing themselves on his thought and feelings; and his religious faith, as it now stands confronted by them, is solemn in its steadfastness rather than triumphant. It is thus that, in his latest utterance, he addresses a new-born child:

> O dear Spirit half-lost
> In thine own shadow and this fleshy sign
> That thou art thou—who wailest being born
> And banished into mystery, and the pain
> Of this divisible-indivisible world,
> Amongst the numerable-innumerable
> Sun, sun, and sun, thro' finite-infinite space
> In finite-infinite Time—our mortal veil
> And shattered phantom of that infinite One,
> Who made thee unconceivably Thyself
> Out of His whole World-self and all in all!

In this it is true that the poet's earlier faith asserts itself; but it does so in a changed tone, which betokens that the conditions of religious thought are different from what they were thirty years ago. It verges upon mysticism. He no longer addresses the

> Strong Son of God, immortal Love,

to whom he could say in those days, full of devout conviction—

> Our little systems have their day;
> They have their day and cease to be;
> They are but broken lights of Thee,
> And Thou, O Lord, art more than they.

He can no longer use this language, though he still endeavours to re-convey the meaning of it. And it is this constancy of his faith under saddening and new conditions that seems to us to be the key to his present literary position. The age has changed, but he has remained constant; and instead of being the impassioned exponent of contemporary thought, all he can now do is to bow his head and submit to it.

If this view of him be true, it will follow that we must look on him as, properly speaking, the poet of a completed epoch. This may seem, at first sight, a startling judgment of a man whose genius we believe to be still in its full vigour. But our meaning is less startling than it may seem to be. Though ages pass, their effects do not perish, nor is their inspiration obsolete because its sources are now sealed to us. The case is exactly the reverse of this. Mr. Matthew Arnold has said, in one of his most pregnant apophthegms,

> Deeds in hours of insight willed
> May be through hours of gloom fulfilled;

and what he says of hours may be also said of epochs. The lessons which sight has taught us may be practised, and may increase in use, when sight is for the time withdrawn. The mind of the world, and the mind of England especially, during the particular period we have been speaking of, was undergoing a momentous experience, the wisdom taught by which will long outlive its circumstances. It is that wisdom, or at least the noblest part of it, that Mr. Tennyson has assimilated, and which he has kept alive for all men in his perfect verse. In the present generation his power has not ceased; it has only changed its function. Whereas his greatest work, as we have said, was moulded by a past epoch, it may help to mould a coming one, and to revive the beliefs and feelings it was itself inspired by. There are some elements in it, no doubt, that are perishable, but the larger part of it is enduring; and Mr. Tennyson has said much, that when he said it was new to poetry, which once so said will never become old.

We have one more observation to add,

which will help perhaps to illustrate our main thesis. We have tried to point out that Mr. Tennyson's special function has been to interpret a special period, and that that period has now gone by. The correctness of these views with regard to his literary office will be realised more clearly if we consider who succeeded him in it. His successor, it seems to us, was none other than George Eliot. What Mr. Tennyson's poetry was to the second quarter of our century, George Eliot's novels have been to the third. The aim of both writers has been the same, though their methods have been so very different. They have both chosen as their one constant theme human nature as related to modern thought; and they have tried to reconcile what was highest in the one to what was most deeply true in the other. But the intellectual condition of the world, as the novelist saw it, was not the condition that inspired and nerved the poet. The novelist was living *into* her true period, just as the poet was living *out of* his; and the very influences that have cast a gloom upon the latter have been those that have given her solemn chiaro-oscuro to the former. Mr. Tennyson has ever tried to discern God through the material universe. It is George Eliot's endeavour to show us we can do without Him. Both treat the affections as the chief treasures of life; but Mr. Tennyson makes these the germ of faith, George Eliot makes them the end of it. Mr. Tennyson looks forward to

> Some far-off divine event
> To which the whole creation moves.

Such a vision as this is to George Eliot a fond delusion. For her in the farthest future there is nothing but one blank catastrophe, when

> Human time
> Shall fold its eyelids, and the human sky
> Be gathered like a scroll within the tomb
> Unread for ever.

That all men in the present day, or even many men, share this dark forecast, we do not presume to say. But though it is not the view that masters the present age, it is without doubt the view that distinguishes it. It occupies even those whom it does not conquer, and either by defiance or submission, we have each and all to deal with it. It has been Mr. Tennyson's mission to express faith; it has been George Eliot's to combat with despair. Mr. Tennyson's spirit breathes still in his latest lines. It is true that, as we have said, it has now a wistful sadness in it; but for that very reason it will here help us better to a comparison. The following is from his last volume; it is from the poem of 'De Profundis,' a part of which we have already quoted. He is addressing the human soul at the close of its action here. 'Still,' he says—

> still depart
> From death to death, thro' life to life, and find
> Nearer and ever nearer Him, who wrought
> Not Matter, nor the finite-infinite,
> *But this main miracle, that thou art thou,*
> *With power on thine own act and on the world.*

Let us now turn to George Eliot, and hear her on the same subject. In her novel of 'Middlemarch' she represents a noble nature, starting in life full of lofty ambitions; and the story is the record of their failures. And what is the conclusion that this suggests to the authoress? There is some comfort in it, but it is comfort of infinite sadness. It is nothing more than this:—That vain as life may be, let us not lose heart utterly, for it is not wholly vain. 'That things,' she says, 'are not so ill with you and me as they might have been, is half owing to the number who have lived faithfully a hidden life,

L

and rest in unvisited tombs.' Thus speaks the spirit of the epoch that has succeeded Mr. Tennyson's. To some of the popular writers of the present day their best consolation is the thought that 'things are not so ill with us as they might have been;' their one shield against despair is an icy stoicism, and their one bond of brotherhood is less of hope than of suffering. If it be the mission then of the great poet or artist to express and not to struggle with the spirit of his epoch, it will be hardly matter of wonder if the course of events lately has not been such as to stimulate Mr. Tennyson. That his latter works have had less influence than his former ones, we shall see to be inevitable from the very circumstances of their composition; and the fact is not to be attributed to any failure of the poet's genius. On the contrary, we believe that were Mr. Tennyson, in his present maturity, to be moved back to the years with whose spirit he was most in harmony, he would excel his former self wherever that was possible; and that what he would do would be as great an advance upon what he has done, as 'Rizpah' is upon 'The May Queen' or 'The Grandmother.'

GEORGE ELIOT ON THE HUMAN CHARACTER.[1]

A DISTINGUISHED living author once observed in our hearing, that there was a time when George Eliot's genius seemed to him to be of almost boundless promise. 'I even thought,' he proceeded, 'that some day she might perhaps have equalled Miss Austen.' There are few, we conceive, amongst George Eliot's admirers who would either thank our critic for these liberal hopes, or sympathise with him in his implied disappointment; nor do we ourselves share in the temper of his criticism. We disagree with him, however, not because his judgment was entirely false, but because it was only very partially true. So far as he had viewed the matter, his view was accurate. It is misleading only because its scope was limited. There are few minds which have accomplished much, that to observant eyes have at one time not promised

[1] 'Theophrastus Such.' By George Eliot. London and Edinburgh: 1879.

more. Even the most many-sided genius must have given hints, at the outset, of the possession of many powers it could never bring to perfection; and we shall often best estimate a writer's chief achievements by examining first the extent and the nature of his partial failures. When, therefore, it is said that George Eliot might have been a second Miss Austen, and has failed to be so, we need not, in assenting to this, be passing a degrading judgment. We advance instantly from our notice of the success she has foregone, to inquiring what other success she has tried to achieve instead of it—what greater birthright she has bought by the sacrifice of her mess of pottage. This inquiry is not altogether an easy one; and a more significant homage could not be paid to the authoress than to say that it is worth our while, in her case, to make it with seriousness. Her present volume is especially useful, not only because it suggests such a task to us, but also because it will assist us in attempting it.

The most obvious aspect under which we look at her is that simply of a novelist—as a dramatic artist in prose. It is not here that her real pre-eminence lies; but we will confine ourselves at first to this very restricted view of her, and regard her as though she were simply a novelist among novelists.

Now, the qualities that a novelist most requires are, in their own degree, the same as those required by a dramatist. A novel, like a drama, is a work of art, and must, like a drama, conform to certain artistic laws, and present certain artistic qualities. The most prominent of these have their close analogies in painting. The first requirements in a picture are that it conform to certain rules of composition, grouping, chiaro-oscuro, and perspective. In like manner we require first of all in a novel or a drama that there be a certain method, grace, and unity in the plot. The various incidents must be presented to us in their due proportion. The attention must not be distracted by unnecessary figures or events. Everything must be properly subordinate to some central interest; and form parts of a single organic whole. When the novelist or the dramatist fulfils these requirements, we may say, in painters' language, that the *composition* of his piece is perfect. As equally apposite examples of this kind of perfection, we may cite two works, which, in other ways, are of a widely different character—'Tom Jones,' and the 'Œdipus Tyrannus' of Sophocles. But *composition* is not all. We require moral perspective and moral chiaro-oscuro as well. What is trivial and incidental must not be drawn too large. What is important must not be drawn too small. And further, the lights and shades, or, if we like to add a new metaphor, the colours, must be properly harmonised and distributed. Everything must not be made an unrelieved darkness by vice or sorrow, or a flat and even brightness by joy or virtue. The novelist and the painter have each of them a kindred artistic effect to produce with shine and shadow, and with various combinations of colour.

Further, there is a second class of requirements needful for a novelist, which might also, were there occasion for it, be illustrated by a reference to painting; and this is an insight into the human heart which is not only profound, but at the same time wide and impartial; and a power, not alone of describing character, but still more of presenting it in action.

If we judge George Eliot's work by the tests above suggested, there is scarcely one adverse criticism to which it is not open. The *composition* of her stories is to the utmost rude and faulty; or rather, in the artistic sense of the word, there is no composition in them at all. In 'Middlemarch,' for instance, we have not one plot, but two, and these joined together in the clumsiest and most unskilful fashion. Elsewhere, it is true, her designs may have more unity; but the unity, even where most traceable, is obscured or quite distorted by masses of irrelevant detail. Every stone in her building may be of marble, and of marble finely cut: but the building as a whole is not fitly framed together; and many of the blocks which exhibit the finest carving are not only not needed by the structure, but they overload it and destroy its symmetry. She recognises the time-worn truth that a story must have a beginning, a middle, and an end; but between these three parts she observes no just proportion. Her action moves onwards by fits and starts. She hurries when we would have her linger: she lingers when we would have her hurry: and her pace seems to depend not so much on the nature of the road, as on the flowers she desires to pluck by the side of it, or the views of distant scenery which she leans over gates to contemplate.

But there is a greater defect still to notice. In dealing with her principal characters she does not, as a general rule, so much *present* them, as *describe* them to us. And we are made all the more keenly conscious of this, because with her minor characters her procedure is exactly opposite. Mrs. Tulliver and Aunt Pullet, discussing a bonnet, are presented to us. Maggie and Stephen Guest, in their love scenes, are described to us. The former group is a painting left to speak for itself. The latter is a charcoal sketch, with a long explanation under it. We are not saying that the sketch may not show higher powers than the painting : but they are not powers of the same order ; they are not the powers we expect to find in an artist. And so far as artistic success—the success of the true novelist—goes, it is not too much to say that with George Eliot this varies in an inverse ratio to the importance which she herself attaches to her subjects.

It will be recollected that in making these remarks we are purposely narrowing our view. We are regarding the authoress under only one aspect. And if our judgment should seem to be somewhat too severe, it is she herself who is responsible for the severity. We are trying her by standards that she has herself suggested; and those standards are the highest. We are condemning the faults of what she has done by the perfection of what she shows us she might have done. She might have been a second Miss Austen: and that within its limits is no small praise; for it means at any rate that she might have been an almost faultless artist. And it is only because we see her to have been capable of perfect art, that we are forced to note the imperfections of the art she has actually given us.

But if she has failed as a novelist where novelists of less genius have succeeded, she exhibits powers to which, amongst other novelists, we can hardly find a parallel, and which only very rarely have expressed themselves in prose fiction at all. She may be less than Miss Austen in art, but she is greater than Scott in insight. Indeed, to compare her even to Scott is an unfairness to her. We must go for our parallel yet a stage higher; and we must not stop short of the world's greatest poets. The art of the novelist, and presumably his vision also, rests on the surface of life and of society. His eyes, so far as he can use them, may be as keen and piercing as the poet's; but he uses them from a different point of view. The varied human landscape lies before him, and he paints what he sees of it; but he is not, like the poet, at a sufficient height above it, to see to the bottom of its deep ravines and valleys, or to the summits of its lofty mountains. That it has deep valleys and that it has mountain peaks, he presumes; but he has neither descended to the one, nor scaled the other. With George Eliot, however, the case is different. She, like the poet, takes a more commanding standpoint. Her eyes are occupied with the high and deep places of the human spirit, and the larger and profounder questions of human destiny. For her, as for the poet, life is, as it were, transparent; and she sees the mightiest issues hiding under the most trivial. Her materials for excitement and interest are not the excitements of adventure, with their varieties of surface incident; her materials for tragedy are not murders or escapes from murder, with the manœuvres of criminals and detectives: but they are the inner spiritual events that take place beneath the surface, and of which the outer events are for her the signs merely. Her works partake thus of the quality that separates the poetry of a great drama from the prose of a great novel. The essential difference, for instance, between 'Hamlet' and 'Pendennis' lies in the different level in human life to which the two works pierce. The one reaches to the poetry of life; the other only presumes it, or at best points to it from a distance. But the vision of George Eliot goes straight to it, and encounters it face to face. She has seen and has felt like Sophocles, that

> Full many things are wonderful, but none
> More fearful and more wonderful than man;[1]

and she has seen and felt this with something of the emotion that is common and almost peculiar to the greatest tragic poets.

And yet with all this George Eliot is not a poet; and, putting form altogether out of the question, her works are not poetry. They bear the same relation to poems that a chrysalis does to a butterfly, just before the change. We feel them to be quivering with a life that demands some further development. We feel that something is on the ground that requires to fly, and that is every moment on the point of soaring.

[1] Antigone, 333.

But the wings never unfold themselves. The strength is wanting somewhere by which the prison is to be broken.

Thus, to pass on her work any general literary judgment is a somewhat puzzling task. But going again for assistance to a simile drawn from painting, we may compare her work, not so much to so many separate pictures, as to so many separate canvases, each covered with a number of pictorial fragments—fragments connected together indeed by some thread, inward or outward, of thought or meaning; but neither in conception nor execution fused together into coherent artistic wholes. We have studies for some heroic subject—some great and solemn action—which are instinct with power and genius but in which the figures are grouped ill, and often only partly outlined; and we have this heroic group broken or surrounded by a number of semi-serious figures—not in outline, but painted in solid colour, and with the most masterly and complete finish. Such at least is the impression which her earlier works have made on us. Her manner latterly, it is true, has grown in some ways more congruous; but this is not because she has learnt to finish the whole of her pictures as she once did their secondary parts; but because she has ceased to use her brush at all, and has left the whole in the condition of shadowy sketches.

To the eye, therefore, of purely artistic criticism, George Eliot's work, even at its highest, is full of flaws and blemishes. The world, however, is not made up entirely of artistic critics; and the common sense of the public, with its wise want of fastidiousness, often detects in a writer what there is of genius the better for not detecting what there is lacking in art and skill. And such is the case with George Eliot. She sees truths about life which vast numbers of men and women feel to be true, and which they are grateful to her for having expressed and set before them. She has given definiteness to views which before were dim and vague to them; she has given voice to thoughts and feelings which before were inarticulate. They feel that she has done this for them *somehow*; and *how* they neither know nor care to criticise. Her books are more to them like Bibles than books of mere amusement; and they have been treated and read with a reverence that was perhaps never before accorded to any works of fiction.

Her position is thus sufficiently remarkable; but there is a point about it beyond any we have yet touched upon, which makes it more remarkable still; and this is a point probably, that is little suspected by the larger part of her most earnest and most reverent students. She is the first great *godless* writer of fiction that has appeared in England; perhaps, in the sense in which we use the expression, the first that has appeared in Europe. To say this may sound a paradox or an insult, but it is neither. And this will appear presently, when we have explained the meaning which we attach to the obnoxious word *godless*.

We must remember that generally, up to the present time, human conduct was, amongst serious people, supposed to bear reference, before all things, to some power above ourselves, and of a different nature, to whom our souls belonged, and for whose sake we were bound to keep them pure. And this conception has so penetrated our modern civilisation, that it has been implied in the entire lives and thoughts of numbers who not only never thought of affirming it, but who even posed as deniers of the belief upon which it rested. Shakespeare, for instance, may or may not have been a religious man ; he may or may not have been a Catholic, or a Protestant. But whatever his personal views or feelings may have been, the light by which he viewed life was the light of Christianity. The shine, the shadow, and the colours of the moral world he looked upon, were all caused or cast by the Christian Sun of Righteousness. But now amongst the vast changes that human thought has been undergoing, the sun that we once all walked by has for many eyes become extinguished ; and every energy has been bent upon supplying man with a substitute, which shall have if possible, an equal illuminating power, and at any rate the same power of moral actinism. This substitute at present is, it is true, somewhat nebulous ; but the substance it is composed of is already sufficiently plain. The new object of our duty is not our Father which is in Heaven, but our brothers and our children who are on earth. It is to these alone, according to the new gospel, that our piety is due ; it is indeed to these that all true piety has, in all ages, been ignorantly paid. It is needless to dwell upon this conception longer. Whether we think it sound or hollow, its general character is familiar enough to all of us; and we know that a growing number of men and women around us are adopting it. But it is one thing to adopt a belief in theory—another thing to put it in practice; and again another thing, to receive it, as it were in solution, into our daily thoughts and feelings, so that we not only act and think by it, but also instinctively judge and feel by it. This third stage is the one that is reached latest, and we doubt whether as yet any considerable body of men and women have attained to it. The nearest approach to it, so far as we know, is to be found in the novels of George Eliot: only there even it is not reached perfectly; for the moral standard of the novelist and the rational justification of her own judgments and sympathies, are not present to her mind instinctively, and as matters of course; but they are for ever being consciously emphasised by herself, and for ever being pointed out, more or less directly, to the reader. At any rate, in the world of earnest art, she is the first legitimate fruit of our modern atheistic pietism; and as such, she is an object of extreme interest, if not to artistic epicures, at any rate to all anxious inquirers into human destiny. For in her writings we have some sort of presentation of a world of high endeavour, pure morality and strong enthusiasm, existing and in full work, without any reference to, or help from, the thought of God. *Godless* in its literal sense, and divested of all vindictive meaning, exactly describes her writings. They are without God, not against him. They do not deny, but they silently and skilfully ignore Him. We have the same old liturgies of human faith and action, only they are intercepted and appropriated by a new object, when they seemed to be on their way to the old. The glory and the devotion that was once given to God is transferred silently to man.

The way in which this feat is performed is very remarkable; for the characters she presents us with are suffered rarely, if ever, to hold opinions that are consciously to themselves at all akin to the author's. On the contrary, they are most of them Christian people, with the love of God and the fear of hell presumably before their eyes. But in all their more vital struggles after God, the supernatural element in their beliefs is represented as having no effect on them. It is treated as a husk or shell, concealing, or perhaps sheltering, something more precious than itself; or at best conveying a truth in

M

metaphor through the channel of a sacramental lie. Mr. Tryan, in 'Janet's Repentance,' and Savonarola in 'Romola,' are both of them marked instances of this; and the author's dealing with these characters is exceedingly skilful. Mr. Tryan is a clergyman, passionately devoted to his sacred calling, an ardent disciple of a special school of divinity, and eaten up with the sincerest zeal for souls. And yet the writer contrives to exhibit all that she wishes us to admire in him as resting on a basis with which his religious beliefs have nothing at all to do. In her portrait of Savonarola this treatment is yet more distinguishable and yet more significant. His chief connection with the story in which she introduces him, is his conversion of the heroine, from the neo-paganism of the Renaissance, to the precepts of Christ, and to a humble acceptance of sorrow. But in all his exhortations to her, and they are some of them singularly beautiful, there is hardly one appeal to Christianity on its supernatural side. Savonarola is the spokesman of Humanity made divine, not of Deity made human. In so far as he is not this, but the reverse of this, there, according to George Eliot, lies his weakness and not his strength. The 'higher life,' the withdrawal from man for the sake of communion with God, is for her a diseased weakness, if not a wickedness. The Christ of the Christian Church says, 'If a man love father and mother more than me, he is not worthy of me.' The Christ of George Eliot says the exact opposite: 'A man is not worthy of me unless he love me less than father or mother.' With her, as she says often and explicitly, the 'transcendent morality' is to share willingly in the 'common lot,' and not to seek escape from ties 'after those ties have ceased to be pleasant.' She urges with a solemn eloquence, she seems to see in a solemn ecstasy, that a man's highest life is to be found in sorrow borne for the sake of others; and that all seeming miseries may be turned to blessings, by making an offering of them to something beyond ourselves. But an offering to what? To the God who has made us, loved us, and suffered for us, and into whose presence we may one day win admission? To no such God; but to some impersonal cause, some force of human progress. 'Make your marriage-sorrows,' says Savonarola, to Romola, 'an offering, too, my daughter: an offering to *the great work* by which sin and sorrow are to be made to cease.' This is the one teaching of all her novels; and its fundamental difference from the higher Christian teaching lies in this, that it asserts the part to be greater and more complete than the whole; that it asserts those human hopes, and loves, and enthusiasms which Christianity has developed for us, and bequeathed to us. to be in reality complete in themselves, and clogged and weighted only, not supported by, what were once supposed to be their divine foundations.

This fact, as we have said before, is probably little suspected by the majority of George Eliot's readers. These carry with them the lamp of their own religion into that tender but gloomy world into which the author leads them; and do not perceive what the only light is, with which it would be else provided. They have themselves supplied what is wanting before they have felt the want. And they have imagined that the beliefs which they do not find dwelt upon, have been pre-supposed as true, instead of being studiously ignored as false. But if we would really see George Eliot in all her full significance, we must not close our eyes thus. If we do, we shall not only miss the one thing which she has renounced much to teach us; but we shall miss something that is of an importance far more general. We shall miss the first concrete examples of the workings of the new religion of humanity ; and the only means as yet offered us by which to test the results of it, as seen or anticipated by one of its own apostles. Further, if we look at her in this way, and with this intention, her work, which seems so chaotic when judged by any mere artistic tests, becomes congruous and intelligible. It is not so much a series of novels, interspersed with philosophical reflections ; it is a gradual setting forth of a philosophy and religion of life, illustrated by a continuous succession of diagrams. That this is the true view of the matter has been getting more and more evident as the career of the author has proceeded. How far this line of development has been conscious and intentional, with herself, it is not ours to inquire. But, consciously or unconsciously, the main stream of her powers has drifted into the philosophic channel, and has left her artistic powers as a mere auxiliary to these, although from the very nature of the case closely connected with them. It is, therefore, by her philosophy that she has the strongest claim to be judged.

Now, it is not our intention here (for neither place nor space permit of it) to discuss that philosophy with reference to its truth or permanent value. But for reasons that will appear presently it will be well to glance at certain salient features of it. The first article of her creed is—I believe in Humanity as the embracer of every moral end that is possible for man; as the only and sufficient object of his highest hopes, and his truest religious emotions. And it is her aim, conscious or unconscious, throughout all her writings to exhibit to us the highest lives directed and nourished only by motives that are purely human. One thing therefore is at once evident. She does not, if we recollect rightly, profess herself to be an optimist. We think indeed she has expressed her convictions somewhere as a creed of '*meliorism.*' But at any rate the whole fabric of her system and her emotions rests, for its one foundation, on a profound satisfaction in the fact of the human race existing, and an earnest hope and expectation of a blessed, if not of a quite perfect, future for it. It is an unspeakable good that it exists now; it will be a yet more unspeakable good that it exists by-and-by.

We need not, however, seek to define her hopes too exactly. It is sufficient that her entire philosophy is an impassioned protest against pessimism, and that it presents the human life and the human lot to us as worthy of all our piety—all our love and reverence. The question that at once arises is, how far does this Deity, as she presents it to us, justify or excite the adoration that she is so pressing we should accord to it? And the answer to this question is somewhat startling. George Eliot, as we have said, is theoretically no pessimist; and yet the picture she presents to us of the world we live in almost exactly answers to the description given of it by Schopenhauer, as nothing better than a 'penal settlement.' It might at first sight seem hard to account for this inconsistency. It might seem that her philosophic theories and her true natural vision were at hopeless war with one another; and that her diagrams refuted instead of illustrating the text of her proposition. Or we might figure her as labouring under a destiny the exact reverse of Balaam's; and having resolved to bless the human destiny, finding herself constrained by the power of truth to curse it.

For in what light is it that she exhibits men

to us? She exhibits them as, first and before all things, beings who are not isolated, but linked together by countless ties of duty and affection; and the essence of all right conduct, and the moral *raison d'être* of existence, consists, according to her, in our willingly keeping these ties inviolate. Thus far the matter does not sound unpromising. But if we go farther, it will appear that the race of beings that are thus linked together, form no happy and rejoicing brotherhood, finding each a glad reward in the sense that the rest are helped by him; but a sad and labouring race of chained convicts, whose highest glory it is not to attempt escaping. We are all born, she teaches, with bonds about us, and we inevitably increase their number, prompted by our own cravings, as we live on. And, says George Eliot, every such bond 'is a debt: the right lies in the payment of that debt; *it can lie nowhere else.* In vain will you wander over the earth; you will be wandering away for ever from the right.'

Now 'the right' according to her teaching, has two distinct characteristics; in the first place, it is the hardest thing of all to attain; and in the next place it is the only thing that is worth attaining. But when it is attained it seems, as she describes it, little better, at the best, from the human stand-point, than a choice between evils. 'Renunciation,' she says explicitly, 'does not cease to be a sorrow; but it is a sorrow borne willingly.' And again she says in another place, 'the highest happiness . . . often brings so much pain with it that we can only tell it from pain by its being what we would choose before everything else, because our souls see it is good.' But thus far clearly she must be doing it some injustice. For elsewhere a sense of positive rapture is supposed to be a part of its content; and despite all its anguish, it is supposed to admit us to some 'vision, that makes all life below it dross for ever.' The matter is a mystery, and is seen by herself to be so; so much so, indeed, that the illustration and simplification of it is really the one purpose that runs through all her novels. The central action of all of them—at least of all the later ones—is transparently the same. It is the choice or the refusal of some person or persons of this highest happiness, which can hardly be told from pain, but which, when once chosen, is to make all else dross for ever. And by these examples she seeks to convince us of three things : firstly, that the *right*, for its own sake, and resting on a strictly human basis, does practically bring its own reward with it, in the way her system requires of it ; secondly, that men and women will recognise this truth, without any bias derived from supernatural hopes or affections ; and, lastly, we gather her to imply that though the number of these loftier natures be but small, they yet supply a kind of vicarious value and sanctity to the entire race they belong to : and thus give ground to the philosopher for a solemn piety towards that race as it is, and a sure if anxious hope for it as it will be.

Now, as this philosophy of George Eliot's is the most rational and moving statement of all that, according to many modern thinkers, the salvation of man depends on, it becomes a matter of no small interest to enquire on what basis of fact she rests it. She certainly does not rest it—and this is the grand point in its favour—on an ignorance or careless observation of life's meanness, sins, and miseries. She does not underestimate the causes for despair. The question is, does she over-estimat the causes for hope? In other words, how far does this prophetess of humanity understand and present correctly the realities of human nature?

The answer to this question is, we fear, not reassuring. We have already pointed out in her work certain artistic anomalies which are fatal to it from the point of view of the artist; and chief amongst these was the strange want of unity in her manner, which we compared to a mixing together of finished figures in oil with shadowy charcoal outlines. Looking at her simply as a novelist, this phenomenon was puzzling. Looking at her as a philosopher, it becomes, we conceive, sufficiently explicable. In her side characters we see her genuine artistic vision, her genuine artistic powers. We see living men and women presented to us with all the power of a dramatist. But when we pass from her side characters to her principal ones, the whole spectacle changes. We have not what the artist discovers as existing, but what the theorist dreams of as that which ought to exist. We have the phantoms of the philosopher projected into the world of reality. In other words, her higher characters, which she holds up to us as the salt of the earth and the examples of right action, are hardly, as she presents them to us, human characters at all. They are principles, not incarnate in so many different bodies, but dressed up in different suits of clothes, and set working under different circumstances. Romola, except in externals, is the same as Dorothea; so too, towards the end of her history, is Maggie Tulliver. This last character, by the way, is in one respect a very curious one. She is a composite product of both of the author's methods. She is begun according to one, she is finished according to the other. She is begun as a little flesh-and-blood girl; she is gradually sublimated into a great philosophy in action. And amongst such shadowy presences, which alone are to be our models and our encouragements, Aunt Gleg moves as Dante did through the world of spirits —a solid body and casting a human shadow, and which we feel at once to belong to quite a different order of beings.

The treatment by George Eliot of her own genius may be compared to her treatment, just noticed, of the character of Maggie Tulliver. There were two tendencies always visible in her

—that of the artist, and that of the philosopher. Could the first of these have absorbed and employed the second, the highest artistic work might doubtless have been the result. As a matter of fact, the philosophy has gained the day; and, as the philosophy has grown, the art has dwindled. But, like Pharaoh's lean kine, it has not fattened by what it has fed upon. Her view of human nature as a philosopher has grown wider than it would have been as an artist; but as it has grown wider it has grown less accurate; and as her inductions have grown more confident, the basis on which she rests them has become less reliable. To make such systems as hers of any practical value, two things are needed. One is a knowledge of the great general principles of human impulse; the other is a knowledge of the various complex circumstances under which these impulses act upon us, and by which their power is profoundly modified. It is this latter sort of knowledge in which George Eliot appears to us to be so deficient. She reminds us of an engineer or a shipwright, who may be well versed in the laws of motion, but who knows little of the practical difficulties caused by friction, or of the various strengths and consistencies of the only materials in which his designs can be carried out. And the shadowy and unreal impression which her typical characters convey to us, we take to be but the outward sign of a fundamental unreality in her conception of them.

Her present volume more than any of the preceding ones serves at once to confirm and to illustrate this impression. Its scope and character fit it in a peculiar way to show us what her general knowledge of the world really is; and in what manner and from what fields she has gleaned the facts on which she supports her theories. And thus, whatever may be its intrinsic interest, it may form for each reader a text for more interesting inquiry. The 'Impressions of Theophrastus Such' belongs to that class of literature which Theophrastus the Greek originated, and which La Bruyère in modern times has made yet more famous. Like the 'Characters' of these two writers, it consists, not of a dramatic presentation of various men acting and reacting with their various aims and powers upon one another, but of studies of men and women taken singly, and regarded primarily in relation to themselves, or rather to a single class of which they are supposed typical, and which is further supposed to be an important element in the composition of society. The talents required by this kind of composition are fewer than those required by the novelist; but though the novelist requires other talents in addition to these, he first and before all things requires these also. Theophrastus and La Bruyère might not have all the makings in them of great novelists: but a great novelist must have all the makings of a Theophrastus or a La Bruyère. The generalised facts that such writers as these present to us, are the raw material of artistic fiction; and George Eliot, in following in their wake, has been inviting us to see the quality of her material before it has been manufactured, and allowing us, perhaps a little unwisely, to examine its quality when in that condition. In the creations of the novelist which are presented to us in rapid action, and which distract our judgment by a vivid appeal to our interest, there may be many defects that will readily escape notice. But in a work like the present, we have the characters standing still as it were, and an examination of them becomes a much simpler task. Further, we are in the present case not only shown what the author thus observes of men, but we are told by her how she observes them, and with what intentions.

Now, in the book before us it is hardly necessary to say that there are many passages that bear the full stamp of the author's insight and originality; but nothing she has ever written has, whilst reminding us of her strength, so fully convinced us of her weakness. In the first place, at the very threshold, we are met with an instance of her want of art—of a sense of what is and what is not superfluous. Her first two chapters are devoted to a description by himself of a certain imaginary bachelor, who tells us he has clumsy feet, a shambling ungainly gait, a frightful upper lip, and an aspect generally that makes ladies smile when they look at him; and it is to this shadowy being that all the following studies of life are attributed. In the character of this gentleman there is nothing very striking or attractive; but the chief fault to find with him is, not that he is vague and vapid, but that he is absolutely unneeded. We suppose him at the outset to have some significance in connection with what follows: but so far as we can see, he has none whatever. He is introduced by the author probably as a sort of screen for her own personality; but her device is none the less inartistic because it was a becoming modesty that suggested it. Nor is it redeemed as art because the bachelor's autobiography is the occasion in one place of one of the finest and most truthful passages in the book, which we think it will not be amiss to present here to the reader. The bachelor is speaking of the changes in English scenery which the progress of the present century had brought with it, 'in contrast,' he says, 'with those grander and vaster regions of the earth, which keep an indifferent aspect in the presence of man's toil and devices.'

What (he continues), does it signify that a Lilliputian train passes over a viaduct amidst the abysses of the Apennines, or that a caravan laden with a nation's offerings creeps across the unresting sameness of the desert, or that a petty cloud of steam sweeps for an instant over the face of an Egyptian colossus, immovably submitting to its slow burial beneath the sand? But our woodlands and pastures, our hedge-parted corn-fields and meadows, our bits of high common where we used to plant the windmills, our quiet little rivers here and there fit to turn a mill-wheel, our villages along the old coach roads, are all easily alterable lineaments that seem to make the face of our Motherland

sympathetic with the laborious lives of her children. . . .
Our rural tracts—where no Babel-chimney scales the heavens
—are without mighty objects to fill the soul with the sense
of an outer world unconquerably aloof from our efforts. . . .
The grasses and reeds nod to each other over the river, but
we have a canal close by; the very heights laugh with corn
in August, or lift the plough-team against the sky in September.
Then comes a crowd of burly navvies with pickaxes
and barrows; and while hardly a wrinkle is made in the
fading mother's face or a new curve of health in the blooming
girl's, the hills are cut through or the breaches between them
spanned; we choose our level, and the white steam pennon
flies along it.

But because our land shows this readiness to be changed,
all signs of permanence upon it raise a tender attachment,
instead of awe. Some of us, at least, love the scanty relics
of our forests, and are thankful if a bush is left of the old
hedgerow. A crumbling bit of wall, where the delicate ivy-leafed
toad-flax hangs its light branches, or a bit of grey
thatch, with patches of dark moss on its shoulder and a
troop of grass-stems on its ridge, is a thing to visit. And
then the tiled roof of cottage and homestead, of the long
cow-shed where generations of the milky mothers have stood
patiently, of the broad-shouldered barns, where the old-fashioned
flail once made resonant music, while the watch-dog
barked at the timidly venturesome fowls making
pecking raids on the outflying grain; the roofs that have
looked out from among the elms and walnut-trees, or beside
the yearly group of hay and corn stacks, or below
the square stone steeple, gathering their grey or ochre
tinted lichens and their olive-green mosses, under all ministries,—let
us praise the sober harmonies they give to our
landscape, helping to unite us pleasantly with the elder
generations.

This eloquent passage is worthy of George Eliot at her best, and not only shows us how on occasions thought and feeling can be harmoniously fused together by her, and presented to us in the form of a vivid picture, but it shows how near she can rise towards the true sublime. What can be more impressive than the first sentence we have quoted, with its solemn presentation of the littleness of man's greatest labours, when confronted with the vaster aspects of Time and Nature? What more skilful than her transitions to the converse picture? Whilst, when we read how the heights lift the plough-team against the sky, prose seems to be standing on tip-toe, and to be on the point of unfolding the wings of poetry.

But we are delaying too long the main subject of our consideration. The chief aspect under which we are to consider our author—the special aspect under which in her new volume she explicitly presents herself, is that of a philosopher and a woman of the world, who has fitted herself to be the former of these by having first become the latter; who claims to speak with authority about man from her intimate knowledge of the ways and works of men.

Deducting the two chapters we have just noticed, the 'Impressions of Theophrastus Such' consists of sixteen essays, of which five or six may be classified as fragments of moral philosophy, and the remaining ten or eleven as studies of the facts of character. Or—for this division is in some way not entirely accurate—we may describe the sixteen essays taken all together as composed of three separate elements, theories, reflections, and observations.

The theories of the author are precisely those we should have expected to find. They are nothing but re-statements of the great thesis of our modern moralised humanism, that the basis and the motive of all right conduct depends on nothing but the necessities of human welfare and the constitution of the human character. To one important side of this theory the whole of her last essay is devoted—the identification of the individual consciousness with the corporate consciousness of the race. She is—and we are glad to see her so far moderate—convinced that we are not at present ripe for a full cosmopolitanism—for a participation in a universal human consciousness. But a participation in a national consciousness, which we are ripe for, is she holds, a far more solid and important fact than we most of us take it to be. 'Not only,' she says, 'does the nobleness of a nation depend on the presence of this national consciousness, but *also the nobleness of each individual citizen.*' The memory of our historical past, the anticipation of our historical future—here is one of the substitutes for the love and the fear of God, and the aspiration after a more intimate communion with him! And the Jews are, in this essay, held up to us as an example of its working power, and the splendid results that would, in their case, come of it, if only the Gentile world were less cynical and selfish.

In her essay on 'Moral Swindlers' the above doctrine is inculcated under a different guise, and with more practical force. In it she comments on the excuses made and the pity expressed for the disgraced director of certain bubble companies, on the ground that he was 'a thoroughly *moral* man.'

'What do you mean by a thoroughly moral man?' said I.
'Oh, I suppose that every one means the same by that,' said Melissa, with a slight air of rebuke. 'Sir Gavial is an excellent family man, quite blameless there; and so charitable round his place at Tiptop. Very different from Mr. Barabbas, whose life, my husband tells me, is most objection-

able, with actresses and that sort of thing. I think a man's morals should make a difference to us. I'm not sorry for Mr. Barabbas, but I *am* sorry for Sir Gavial Mantrap.'
. . . I wish that this narrow use of words, which are wanted in their full meaning, were confined to women like Melissa. Seeing that Morality and Morals under their *alias* of Ethics are the subject of voluminous discussion, and their true basis a pressing matter of dispute, . . . one might expect to find that educated men would avoid a perversion of language which lends itself to no wider view of life than that of village gossips. . . . Not for one moment would one willingly lose sight of the truth that the relation of the sexes and the primary ties of kinship are the deepest root of human well-being; but to make them by themselves the equivalent of morality is verbally to cut off the channels of feeling through which they are the feeders of that well-being.

The writer proceeds to explain her meaning farther, by declaring that the most momentous portion of morality, and that to which the name should be most emphatically applied, lies not in personal purity of life, or benignity and self-restraint towards those about us, but in what she calls 'good workmanship . . . manipulative or other,' from—and these are her own examples—the making a pair of boots to the editing a political newspaper. And the one thing needful, she says, to the loftiest moral life, and—as she elsewhere adds—to the only true religion as well, is 'an effective and awe-inspiring vision of the human lot,' and an understanding of 'the connection between duty and the material processes by which the world is kept habitable.'

How far all this will harmonise with certain of her other dicta we cannot here pause to inquire. We should have conceived, however, from certain passages in her writings, and from many incidents in her stories, that the inner intention which an act embodied, and not the material results that followed on it, were, according to her view, the primary tests of morality; and that actions might, at times, be in the highest sense moral, though their inevitable results could be nothing but unhappiness. The question, however, is not whether one view of the question is true, and another false; for they are not mutually exclusive; on the contrary, they each imply the other, and no moralist for a moment ever doubted the truth of either of them. The only question is as to their relative importance. It is not whether private morality is possible without public, but whether public morality is possible without private; and whether private morality, with the agonising struggles which she says are involved in it, can be ever generally sustained by merely temporal aspirations and enthusiasms.

Morality must spring, she tells us, from an 'effective and awe-inspiring vision of the human lot.' That possibly may be very true: but is the 'human lot' calculated to inspire awe? Doubtless it is so for those who suppose that each human being has a stake in eternity. Will it be equally so for those who suppose man's greatest mission is to 'keep the world habitable' for himself and his ephemeral children? Will the 'vision' supply such men with the solemn enthusiasm and the severe resolve that will alone serve their purpose? This is really the long and short of the matter. The whole philosophic dispute becomes at last eminently practical; and is carried inevitably from that lower court in which cases are judged by theory, to that higher and final one, where they are judged by homely knowledge of the world and shrewd observation of fact. The 'common lot,' as it exists at present, can be an object of 'effective vision' for George Eliot, only as containing in itself the seeds of its own improvement. At present the world consists of a majority that have need to be improved, and of a minority that are labouring to improve them; but if mankind show few signs of progress, not only does their own existence become morally hopeless, but the efforts of their improvers become altogether vain. Does our author, then, really see in the world around her any sure signs for the faith that she feels and inculcates? Is the awe that the 'vision' inspires her with due to the width of her view, or to a haze that distance lends to it? Let us turn from her generalisations on man to the specimens she offers us of typical individual men.

We used to question whether in the whole range of fiction there was ever a being so unreal and so meaningless as the gentleman or the man of fashion described by Dickens. Certainly no chimæra or centaur could be more impossible than Sir Mulberry Hawk or Lord Frederick Verisopht. But George Eliot has, we think, equalled Dickens. If Sir Mulberry Hawk and Lord Frederick are chimæras, the men and women of 'Theophrastus Such' are wraiths. They are intended to be typical human beings, but they are hardly human beings at all. They are like shapes seen in a dream, which seem always on the point of speaking, but which never utter a sound, and which grow more faint and shadowy the more we look at them. We cannot, indeed, call them impossible, as we could

Sir Mulberry Hawk, for they are not definite enough to have so definite a judgment pronounced on them. On the contrary, so far as we can judge of them. they are not only not impossible, but they are not improbable. As we read the descriptions of them, our impression is that the author must have had some reality in her mind; but if the reader would get at this reality, his imagination has so far to amend what she presents him with, that the result will be to his credit rather than hers; and when the result is attained, and the faint and timid outlines are filled in so as to somewhat approach a portrait, his chief feeling will be wonder that such portraits should have been thought worth taking. There are descriptions in these essays, of at least twenty characters, every one of which is meant to be typical of some important element in society, and is expressly used to point some important moral. But it is not too much to say that in not one of those characters is there the least sense conveyed to us of the author's having really *seen* her subjects, or at any rate having been in any degree familiar with them. They are like the productions of one who has thought much about life, but has known practically very little of it; and who has seen the less of it, the more she has come to think about it. Very different is she in this way from her two illustrious predecessors. The qualities most present in them are precisely those most absent in George Eliot. Theophrastus and La Bruyère both impress us instantly as men with a profound knowledge of life. They may or may not have used this knowledge as the foundation of philosophic theories; but there, at all events, is the hard knowledge of facts, without which all the theories will be valueless. They do not inform us whether they have had any 'awe-inspiring visions' of man; but they show us, without telling us, that they have had a very keen vision of men. Two thousand years and more have passed since the days of Theophrastus, and yet his characters are as vivid as though they were painted yesterday. As we study them the past seems present; the dead world seems alive again. Generations divide us from La Bruyère, and a part of his salt, it is true, has lost its savour with time. But this is a part that we can well spare. What remains fresh, is fresh and pungent as on the day he wrote it.

'Theophrastus Such' impresses us in a way precisely opposite. Instead of making the past seem near to us, it makes the present seem remote. And it does this in two ways; firstly, in the manner in which the facts are presented to us; secondly, in the facts that are selected for presentation. The manner is timid, dreamlike and shadowy, where it should be wide-awake and familiar. The facts, when they should be typical of what is of wide importance, are typical only of what is most trivial or confined in interest; or when not that, they are without any meaning whatever, unless we are to suppose them to be undiscoverable personalities. Let us take the following description, for instance, of a gentleman called Spike, who is given us as a type of what the author calls a 'political molecule:'—

He was (she says), a political molecule of the most gentlemanlike appearance, not less than six feet high, and showing the utmost nicety in the care of his person and equipment. His umbrella was especially remarkable for its neatness, though perhaps he swung it unduly in walking. His complexion was fresh, his eyes small, bright and twinkling. He was seen to great advantage in a hat and great coat—garments frequently fatal to the impressiveness of shorter figures; but when he was uncovered in the drawing room it was impossible not to observe that his head shelve off too rapidly from the eyebrows towards the crown, and that his length of limb seemed to have used up his mind so as to cause an air of abstraction from conversational topics. He appeared, indeed, to be preoccupied with a sense of his exquisite cleanliness, clapped his hands together and rubbed them frequently, straightened his back, and even opened his mouth and closed it again with a slight snap, apparently for no other purpose than the confirmation to himself of his own powers in that line. . . . Sometimes Spike's mind, emerging from its preoccupation, burst forth in a remark delivered with smiling zest; as that he did like to see gravel walks well rolled, or that a lady should always wear the best jewellery, or that a bride was a most interesting object; but finding these ideas received rather coldly, he would relapse into abstraction, draw up his back, wrinkle his brows longitudinally, and seem to regard society, even including gravel walks and brides, as essentially a poor affair.

Now, for what purpose is this vapid phantom conjured up for us? To illustrate what truth? The truth, that political demands which are made by the individual selfishly are often 'transmuted by the nature of things' into 'a demand for the public benefit.' Now, we should have ourselves thought this a truism so obvious that it required no more illustration than the fact that a man sleeps when he is sleepy, and so ceases to keep others awake who happen to be sleepy also. But even were anything gained by the illustration here offered us—that of a narrow-minded cotton-spinner, who with a keen insight into no political truths save a few that bear on his own commercial interests, is yet an involuntary helper to his brothers in commerce also, the portrait of this special cotton-spinner adds nothing to our understanding of the lesson Spike himself is as much a superfluity as in a diagram of a pump would be a picture of a man at the handle; and his place and function might be signified just as well by a single capital letter as by the vague and long-drawn description of him we have just quoted. Where, we ask, was the need of all those particulars? Would not the picture have been equally useful, or useless had every feature in it been reversed: had Spike been a dwarf instead of six feet high, had his eyes been languid instead of bright and sparkling and had he thought that brides looked sheepish rather than interesting? Let us contrast this description of George Eliot's with one of La Bruyère's, in which the effect is produced in precisely similar way—an enumeration of external details as to manner and deportment:—

Giton a le teint frais, le visage plein, et les joues pendantes, l'œil fixe et assuré, les épaules larges, l'estomac haut la démarche ferme et délibérée; il parle avec confiance, fait répéter celui qui l'entretient, et il ne goûte que médiocrement tout ce qu'il lui dit ; il dort le jour, il dort la nuit, et profondément ; il ronfle en compagnie ; il occupe à table et à la promenade plus de place qu'un autre ; il tient le milieu en se promenant avec ses égaux ; il s'arrête, et l'on s'arrête ; il continue de marcher, et l'on marche ; tous se règlent sur lui ; il interrompt, il redresse ceux qui ont la parole ; on ne l'interrompt pas, on l'écoute aussi longtemps qu'il veut parler, on est de son avis ; on croit les nouvelles qu'il débite. S'il s'assied, vous le voyez s'enfoncer dans un fauteuil, croiser les jambes l'un sur l'autre, froncer le sourcil, abaisser son chapeau sur ses yeux pour ne voir personne, ou le relever en suite, et découvrir son front, par fierté ou par audace. Il est enjoué, grand rieur, impatient, présomptueux, colère, libertin, politique, mystérieux sur les affaires du temps ; il se croit des talents et de l'esprit :—il est riche !

What a difference between the two styles of portraiture. In La Bruyère's every detail tells —in George Eliot's none. Everything in the former is typical of a class ; all that we can say of the latter is that some things in it may be accidents of some special individual. Let us make another comparison. Let us compare Theophrastus Such with Theophrastus, and see how the impressions of the two differ when they are concerned with the same object. The following is the portrait Theophrastus gives of the Flatterer :—

The flatterer is a person who will say when he walks

with another, 'Do you observe how people are looking at you? This happens to no man in Athens but you. A compliment was paid you yesterday in the porch. More than thirty persons were sitting there, and the question was started, Who is our foremost man? Everyone mentioned you first, and ended by coming back to your name.' With these and the like words he will remove a morsel of wool from his patron's coat; or, if a speck of chaff has been laid on the other's hair by the wind, he will pick it off, adding with a laugh, 'Do you see? Because I have not met you for two days, you have had your beard full of white hairs; although no one has darker hair for his years than you.' Then he will request the company to be silent while the great man is speaking, and will praise him, too, in his hearing, and mark his approbation in a pause with 'True;' or he will laugh at a frigid joke, and stuff his cloak into his mouth as if he could not repress his amusement. . . . If his patron is approaching a friend, he will run forward and say, 'He is coming to you;' and then turning back, 'I have announced you.' . . . He is the first of the guests to praise the wine, and to say, as he reclines next the host, 'How delicate is your fare.' . . . He will ask his friend if he is cold, and if he would like to put something more on; and before the words are spoken, will wrap him up. Moreover, he will lean towards his ear and whisper with him; or will glance at him as he talks to the rest of the company. He will take the cushions from the slave in the theatre, and spread them on the seat with his own hands.[1]

Let us compare this with George Eliot's portrait of 'A too deferential Man.' We may first remark, however, that in this case what she

[1] Mr. R. C. Jebb's translation. 1870.

desires to illustrate is a fact requiring really keen observation to detect, and not at all obvious to the careless eye :—

> People are misled (she tells us), by the common mistake of supposing that men's behaviour, whether habitual or occasional, is chiefly determined by a distinctly conceived motive, a definite object to be gained, or a definite evil to be avoided. The truth is that, the primitive want of nature once tolerably satisfied, the majority of mankind, even in civilised life full of solicitations, are with difficulty aroused to the distinct conception of an object towards which they will direct their actions with careful adaptation, and it is yet rarer to find one who can persist in the systematic pursuit of such an end. . . . Society is chiefly made up of human beings whose daily acts are all performed either in unreflecting obedience to custom and routine, or from immediate promptings of thought or feeling to execute an immediate purpose. . . . When they fall into ungraceful compliment, or other luckless efforts of complaisant behaviour, these are but the tricks or habits gradually formed under the successive promptings of a wish to be agreeable, stimulated day by day without any widening resources for gratifying the wish. It does not in the least follow that they are seeking by studied hypocrisy to get something for themselves.

Now, all this, though it is said in a singularly flat and unincisive way, is yet without doubt quite worth saying. But when we turn to the example by which she desires to illustrate it, we can hardly conceive one feebler and less luminous. She calls her 'Too Deferential Man' Hinze.

From his name (she says), you might suppose him to be German; in fact, his family is Alsatian, but he has been settled in England for more than one generation. He is the superlatively deferential man. . . . He cultivates the low-toned *tête-à-tête*, keeping his hat carefully in his hand and often stroking it, as if to relieve his feelings under the pressure of the remarkable conversation which it is his honour to enjoy at the present moment. I confess to some rage on hearing him yesterday talking to Felicia, who is certainly a clever woman; . . . but you would have imagined that Hinze had been prepared by general report to regard his introduction to her as an opportunity comparable to an audience of the Delphic Sibyl. Felicia . . . evidently embarrassed by this reverent wonder, . . . became somewhat confused, stumbling on her answers, rather than choosing them. He continued to put large questions, bending his head slightly, that his eyes might be a little lifted in awaiting her reply.

'What, may I ask, is your opinion as to the state of art in England?'

'Oh,' said Felicia with a slightly deprecatory laugh, 'I think it suffers from two diseases—bad taste in the patrons, and want of inspiration in the artists.'

'That is true, indeed,' said Hinze, in an undertone of deep conviction. 'You have put your finger with strict accuracy on the causes of decline. To a cultivated taste like yours, this must be particularly painful.'

What we have quoted already, is nearly as long as the whole of the corresponding sketch of Theophrastus; and of George Eliot's we have quoted a fifth part only. For seven or eight more pages are the doings and the disposition of Hinze enlarged upon; and our impression of him in the end is if anything more hazy than at the beginning. It is quite possible that the peculiarities she ascribes to him may one and all of them belong to some living individual, but they do not make that individual live for us. They are not characteristic of even a single human being, much less are they typical of any important class; nor do they help us in any degree to understand practically the important general truth which they are intended to illustrate.

The same singular infelicity in the selection of facts to dwell upon is exhibited perhaps even more strongly in the essays called 'So Young,' and 'Diseases of Small Authorship.' The former of these is an account of a man named Ganymede, who was precocious in his boyhood and who looked boyish in his early manhood. He was always taken for younger than he was, and so he cherished the pleasing notion that he was still a youth at forty. This is the sum and substance of the entire essay. How any human being could have thought it worth the writing is more than we can say. In 'Diseases of Small

Authorship,' we have two companion pictures, between which there seems no essential difference beyond the sex of the subjects. The one is of a man, the other of a woman, who have each of them at some time or other written a single book, and who find in that book thereafter their principal pride and topic. This is the one fact that we are told about them. They are nothing but two names, garnished with a few meaningless rags of detail, to which this meaningless fact is attached.

We have already set a sample of George Eliot's work side by side with that of Theophrastus; and the contrast between the two writers hardly needs to be pointed further. Every detail that the Greek gives us is perennially typical of some special character; every character is typical of some perennial class. We can do nothing in George Eliot's case but flatly reverse the criticism. The important difference, however, between the two writers, is no mere difference in literary skill. It lies far deeper; it points to far more important issues; and the other is but the outward and accidental sign of it. It is the difference in their acquaintance with life; in their insight into the practical working capacities of human nature. In just the same way is George Eliot contrasted with La Bruyère; and as most of the powers of Theophrastus are included in his, with the addition of some others, La Bruyère will perhaps be of most service to us in the comparison we are about to enter on.

It will be recollected that the chief question we have been trying to suggest to the reader, is the question of how far George Eliot's knowledge of human nature fits her to be a prophet about its prospects and its general value—how far her 'vision of the human lot' is accurate and authentic. Now, as we have already said, her knowledge in this matter is in some ways both profound and singular. But its value is destroyed by being incomplete and partial. We have compared her already to an engineer who is a full master of certain mechanical theories, but who is in the most naïve ignorance of the strength of engineering materials—who knows little of the action on them of heat and cold, or of the comparative strengths of iron, oak, and steel. She sees the various temptations that beset men, and the various noble impulses that at times stir them; but she does not see in their due proportions what are men's average powers of resisting the one, or their average likelihood of being lifted upwards by the other. It is just in this kind of insight that La Bruyère is so conspicuous. His vision of the human lot is distorted by no theories as to the effect it ought to produce upon him. He sees it as it is, and he shows it as he sees it. In every word he writes, we see that he is at home with his subject. He has that accurate empirical knowledge which, in all practical matters, is the only foundation on which any sound theory can be built. Let us compare the course of humanity to a horse-race ; and La Bruyère, we may say, predicts its issue like a groom or a book-maker ; George Eliot, like an excited poet. It is true that she knows human nature to be weak and wavering ; but this is a knowledge which she never seems properly to assimilate. Just as a cynic knows that virtue exists, and yet trusts human nature no more for it, so does George Eliot know that vice and weakness exist and yet trusts human nature none the less for it. In her present volume, the weaknesses of men are the chief topic dwelt on ; and her treatment of these shows us more clearly than anything else she has written, the reason why her recognition of them is so unproductive. They are all for her things at a distance, seen through a glass darkly; sounds heard in a dream. She is not familiar with them; they do not appeal to her with human everyday voices. She has the same shyness which tries to seem like ease, as she moves amongst them, that a village curate might have when he dined at the great house of his neighbourhood.

Not only the matter of her book shows this but her manner also—a manner indeed which is nothing new to her, but which seems latterly to have grown more and more emphasised. She is stiff and pompous. She cannot say a simple thing simply; she has infinite ingenuity in insinuating platitudes; she says oracularly what was too evident to be worth saying at all; and what was perfectly fit to be said outright and bluntly, she continually hints at with a species of elephantine *archness*. Thus instead of plainly saying of a clergyman that his memory had decayed, and with it his once ripe scholarship, she informs us with a suppressed knowingness that 'there is another stage that is beyond ripeness, and less appreciated in the market.' A living Englishman she calls 'a British subject included in the last census.' A servant's spelling is, in her language, 'unvitiated by non-phonetic superfluities;' and the county aristocracy are 'such of humanity as live within park-railings.' Here again is a piece of wisdom, for which the whole essay, of which, it is the concluding sentence, has been gradually preparing our incredulous and startled ears: 'Let us be just enough to admit that there may be old-young coxcombs as well as old-young coquettes,' she says; as if the former were not known to us just as well as the latter, and had not figured equally often in life, literature, and conversation.

These things in themselves are only trifles; but they are trifles which in the present case mean a great deal. They illustrate that practical inacquaintance of the authoress with society as a working machine, which was already evident to us in other ways; and to which, when she is speaking to us as in eloquent prophecy, we should be wise to pay special attention.

We trust that her admirers will not think we do her injustice; that when pointing out her defects we are forgetting her signal merits; that because we see the feet of the image to be clay, we forget that the head is gold. We do nothing of the kind. Rather, the more strongly we are impressed with her ignorance of life in one sense, the more do we feel and wonder at her knowledge of it in another. In the midst, to use an expression of her own, of her 'maze of illusory discoveries' as to the general ways of men, we come across reflections of quite a different order, like granite boulders on a plain of sand. Take this for instance :—

Men's minds differ in what we may call their climate, or share of solar energy ; and a feeling or tendency which is comparable to a panther in one, may have no more imposing aspect than that of a weasel in another.

It is a pity that the effect of this pregnant sentence is weakened by a number of tame variations on it which come directly after. But what in itself can be more clear and trenchant ! Whilst as to the following, there are few men, we imagine, who will not be touched to some degree by its keen and piercing pathos :

I have sometimes thought that the facility of men in believing that they are still what they once meant to be,—this undisturbed appropriation of a traditional character, which is often but a melancholy relic of early resolutions, like the worn and soiled testimonial to soberness and honesty carried in the pocket of a tippler whom the need of a dram had driven into peculation—may sometimes diminish the turpitude of what seems a flat and barefaced falsehood.

Here again we have a really weighty aphorism :—

> It is not true that a man's intellectual power is like the strength of a timber beam, to be measured by its weakest point.

Instances of this same kind of power might be multiplied almost indefinitely ; but, as we have said already, they do nothing to strengthen our belief in that practical knowledge of mankind which would alone give us confidence in the value of her general theories, her piety towards humanity, her faith in its future progress, and her belief in it as a substitute for every extra-human object of devotion.

We have yet a farther point to notice, and a very curious one. Not only does George Eliot not seem aware of how her theories are really at variance with her more profound reflections on life, and how utterly unsupported they are by what she fancies to be her practical knowledge of it ; but she actually touches herself on the chief and most hopeless flaws in them, and yet seems to be somehow quite unaware that she has done so, or else in nervous haste, to wilfully close her eyes to the fact. We are alluding especially to two essays in her present volume, 'Shadows of the Coming Race,' and 'Debasing the Moral Currency.' In the former, which, as the name suggests, has much in it that is borrowed from Lord Lytton, the author gives us a forecast of a state of things in which the conclusions of modern science shall have become the natural heritage of the world at large, and consciousness shall have been accepted as simply an 'accompaniment' to life, to which 'prejudice' once gave 'a supreme governing rank, when, in truth, it is an idle parasite on the grand sequence of things . . . a futile cargo, screeching irrelevantly, like a fowl tied head downwards to the saddle of a swift horseman.' Now, this is exactly what the scientific school of which George Eliot herself is an avowed disciple proclaims consciousness to be : what she says has the sound only and not the sense of a misrepresentation. And yet at the end, when she supposes herself asked if the above beliefs, with certain others, are hers, ' Heaven forbid !' she replies.

> They seem to be flying about in the air with other germs, and have found a sort of nidus among my melancholy fancies. Nobody really holds them. They bear the same

relation to real belief as walking on the head for a show does to running away from an explosion or walking fast to catch the train.

This may be true enough; but it is no answer to the difficulty. The conclusions which she thinks can be dismissed so easily, she admits are 'logical,' and 'well argued' from the scientific premisses. If this be the case there must be some flaw in the premisses themselves; and if it be true, as she says, that 'nobody really holds' the former, there would be more intellectual candour, more justice done both to herself and others, were she to admit that, in her opinion, nobody really held the latter. But that any such alternative is before her she seems to have no notion. 'Debasing the Moral Currency' suggests reflections to us that are yet more surprising. Our author's most sacred faith, we must remember, is a faith in the permanent preciousness of human nature; and the most precious part of human nature is its noblest and most inspiring sentiments. And yet in the essay to which we are now alluding she informs us in so many words that the most precious part of humanity is also the most perishable.

THE HUMAN CHARACTER 205

These [*i.e.* our highest moral sentiments] are (she says), the most delicate elements of our too easily perishable civilisation. And here, again, I like to quote a French testimony. Sainte-Beuve, referring to a time of insurrectionary disturbance, says : 'Rien de plus prompt à baisser que la civilisation dans les crises comme celle-ci ; on perd en trois semaines le résultat de plusieurs siècles. La civilisation, la *vie* est une chose apprise et inventée, qu'on le sache bien : '*Inventas aut qui vitam excoluere per artes.*' Les hommes après quelques années de paix oublient trop cette vérité : ils arrivent à croire que la *culture* est chose innée, qu'elle est la même chose que la *nature*. La sauvagerie est toujours là à deux pas, et, dès qu'on lâche pied, elle recommence.'

With all this we ourselves concur most heartily ; but it strikes us as coming strangely from one who believes in nothing worthy of devotion outside humanity. We should have thought that with such a believer 'la culture' was essentially 'la même chose que la nature,' and that humanity, once civilised, was as likely to grow savage as a man once old was likely to grow young again. We should have thought that such fears as those above expressed argued a somewhat impious mistrust of the one Deity that it is right and rational for us to serve and worship.

This is not the place, however for a philosophical discussion. We are not writing a critique on the modern cultus of humanity. We have been but endeavouring to point out to the reader what a singular light on that cultus may be thrown by the writings of its most inspired apostle. Against her as a teacher, and a representative teacher, our main charges have been these. Though her general reflections on life are both profound and original, her particular observations of it have been so limited or so hazy, that she possesses no knowledge fit to form a foundation for any scientific theory of it. Her theory, such as it is, is utterly unsupported by the foundation, such as it is. Or, rather, the entire fabric seems to be inverted, and the foundation, turned uppermost, seems to be crushing the superstructure. The new religion, by the light of which she attempts to view life, seems to be the ghost of a Methodistic theism, which has escaped from its old body, and for which she is trying in vain to find a new one. The body she selects is humanity; but she fails to see how unfit that ruinous and polluted temple is for the reception of such an inmate. The reason of this failure on her part is probably due rather to the fineness of her nature than to any deficiency of her intellect; and though it is to her discredit as a philosopher, it is to her credit as a woman. Plato has observed that a physician, if he would obtain a real insight into the nature of disease, should not himself be a man of entirely robust health. In the same way, would a philosopher understand human nature thoroughly, he should, we much fear, be not of the robustest morals. We do not in the least mean that he should be a vicious man, but that he should, at least, have not been always a very virtuous one. Men err in their judgments on human nature, both by being very good and by being very bad. But the knave's estimate of the world is little more faulty than the hero's; indeed, sad as it may be to say it, we fear that very often it is less so—less so, that is, as regards the practical course of things; for most of the knavery that the hero is too good to suspect, is knavery that is successful, and bears fruit in accomplished deeds: whilst most of the good that the knave is too degraded to dream of, is good not as practical success, but merely as heroic failure. We admire Leonidas more than Xerxes; but Leonidas falls, and the Persians pass Thermopylæ. We admire the martyr more than the apostate; yet we suspect that the actual history of Christianity would have been predicted more accurately by the apostate than the martyr. There are few of what she considers the weak features in Christianity on which George Eliot is harder than the ecstatic visions of the monks. And yet these monks, as she herself admits, were men of singular self-devotion, and consumed by passionate enthusiasm. We would ask her to apply to herself her own criticisms, and to inquire whether her 'awe-inspiring visions of the common lot' have more solid substance in them than the monk's visions of his Redeemer.

To criticise the faults and the weakness of what is great and noble is always a painful task. Utterly as we disbelieve in the religion of Humanity, as a system in any way self-sufficient; utterly as we believe it to be at variance with all accurate and all dispassionate observation, we yet cannot refuse to admire those who persist in proclaiming as omnipotent and eternal the goodness which they themselves at times acknowledge to be so perishable; nor, supposing for a moment that immorality and theism are so connected as some writers contend they are, shall we apply inaptly to such theorists as

George Eliot that memorable line, so full of mournful reverence—

> Victrix causa Deis placuit, sed victa Catoni.

And yet clearly, where great fallaciies exist, it is our duty to do our best to expose them, and to extract them from the shadow of the truths under which they shelter. Fortifying ourself against a reverence that may easily become a superstition, it is our duty to contend against the golden falsehoods, the heroic flatteries with which certain philosophers would now disturb our view of the human race. Nor, as a counterblast to George Eliot's eloquence, can we do better than commend to the reader such unheroic, but such true wisdom as that which breathes in the following sentences of La Bruyère:—

> Ne nous emportons point contre les hommes en voyant leur dureté, leur ingratitude, leur injustice, leur fierté, l'amour d'eux-mêmes, et l'oubli des autres. Ils sont ainsi faits, c'est leur nature, c'est de ne pouvoir supporter que la pierre tombe, ou que le feu s'élève. . . . Le stoïcisme est un jeu d'esprit et une idée semblable à la république de Platon.

We have dwelt at length on the fact that George Eliot's theories of the world are not yet borne out by her examples of it. We have pointed out how, though theoretically she is at least a mitigated optimist, her representations of the common lot are those of the most gloomy pessimist. We think that we cannot quit the subject better than in indicating some clue to this seemingly so strange inconsistency. It may be found, we take it, in the following words of her own :—

> No wonder (she says), the sick-room and the lazaretto have so often been a refuge from the tossings of intellectual doubt—a place of repose for the worn and wounded spirit. Here is a duty about which all creeds and all philosophers are at one; here, at least, the conscience will not be dogged by doubt, the benign impulse will not be checked by adverse theory; here you may begin to act without settling one preliminary question.

Exactly so : and George Eliot's device for exhibiting a purely human virtue to us is to represent all life as a sick-chamber, in which her heroes and heroines are the ministrants, and all the rest of the world is dying in ignoble agony. How far such a view of life as this is calculated permanently to stimulate progress and to sustain flagging endeavours, we must leave to be considered by others, and to be discussed in other places.

NATURAL RELIGION.[1]

Some seventeen years ago a singular book was published, which perplexed and startled the religious world of England. It edified some, it shocked others; and for a time left others doubtful whether they ought to be shocked or edified. That book was the celebrated 'Ecce Homo'; nor, when we consider its tone and subject, can we at all wonder at the ambiguous effect produced by it. It professed to be a study of Christ's life and nature, regarded solely under their human aspect. It was conceived, as such, in a spirit of the deepest reverence. Its moral phraseology, though partly that of philosophy, was in a greater measure that of the Christian pulpit. The sacred character which it undertook to analyse, was analysed only that it might be made a clearer object for imitation. The author evidently was in some sense a

[1] By the Author of 'Ecce Homo.' London: 1882.

Christian, and a Christian whose piety was of an unusually earnest kind. The most orthodox readers were obliged to admit all this; and they were not, nor could they be, untouched by its influence. From the very first, however, not the orthodox only, but many whose theology was then looked upon as the broadest, felt a certain suspicion of this new and persuasive teacher; and their suspicions grew to certainties as they studied his work more closely. Christian, in some sense, he no doubt was; but his Christianity, they soon detected, was something distinct from theirs. The distinction, it is true, was nowhere expressly stated by him. He preserved, on the contrary, a solemn and guarded silence about it; and left it to be inferred, or not inferred, by his readers. His true position was thus for a short time doubtful; but it was doubtful to the intelligent for a short time only. They soon detected in his book, under al its moral fervour, not so much a tendency t general theological scepticism as a distinct re pudiation of one doctrine in particular, on whic the whole theology of the Christian world ha based itself. Not only did 'Ecce Homo,' i literal accordance with its title, confine itself t the consideration of Christ's strictly human nature, but it invited the reader so to conceive that nature as to shut out tacitly any real belief in a Divine nature, distinct from and yet united to it. The Christ thus depicted might no doubt be the Holy One; He might no doubt be the first of created things; but He was certainly not the Word by whom all things were created. He was not the Christ of the fourth Gospel; He was not the Christ of the Nicene Creed; He was not the Christ of any of the Christian Churches, Greek, Roman, or Protestant. Critics were not wanting to impress this fact on the public. One of the chief theologians of the High Church party declared the author to be a man who had lost faith. The Evangelicals, and many Broad Churchmen, were committed by their tenets to a precisely similar judgment on him; and of those who divined his drift, none completely welcomed him but the laxest and most heterodox of the religious rationalists.

It is not our purpose here to criticise 'Ecce Homo;' but we have certain reasons for wishing to recall to the reader the intellectual stand-point which the author assumed in writing it, and the kind of influence which it has since exercised and represented. Long before its publication, the battle between science and orthodoxy had spread itself into the field of popular thought and literature. There had been, amongst writers addressing the general public, scientific critics openly at war with orthodoxy; there had been orthodox apologists openly at war with science; there had also been a party, on the same side as the orthodox, who were willing and anxious to come to terms with the adversary. But though it had been attempted by many Christian writers to accommodate the Christian position to the demands of sceptical criticism, sceptical criticism had as yet, in no popular way, attempted to appropriate the Christian position for itself. To do this was the object of 'Ecce Homo.' Unlike the authors of 'Essays and Reviews,' the author of this book approached and treated his subject not from within the Church, but altogether from without it. Like most men of his time, he must have been born in the Christian pale; but it was quite evident that he had formally left this; and he was examining the Gospel now as a new species of convert, not as one who was striving to keep the faith. To some of the Broad Church party, the Church, as assailed by science, seemed merely like a vessel that had been seized by an intellectual custom-house; and their chief occupation was to select and to pitch overboard all the doctrines that science might call in question. But the author of 'Ecce Homo' was possessed of a different aim. It was not to eradicate error from a faith he was resolved to keep, but to find truth afresh in a faith he had already discarded. In this way he performed a work of greater immediate import than he, probably, at that time was conscious of; and he found an audience larger than he had anticipated. Under the cover of a silence which has long since been broken, the ranks of unwilling sceptics were then rapidly swelling. One by one, with sincere reluctance, men were parting with faiths that had been the most cherished things of their childhood; and though they longed to replace them, they were doubtful how to do so. To such men, or at least to a large number of them, 'Ecce Homo' came like a light in darkness. It seemed to say the exact word they were waiting for. It introduced them to a teacher who, equally with themselves, had felt the force of modern destructive criticism. He had boldly allowed it

to do, as he thought, its worst. He had allowed
it to rob him of all accepted theology, of all
membership of any recognised Church ; and yet
in the end, this very same criticism was, as it
seemed, bringing him back to Christ. Here was
a comfort, indeed, to a number of vexed spirits.
Here was a teacher who had been in all points
tried as they had been. He had lost, of his first
beliefs, all that they had lost. He not only had
no faith left in the Mosaic account of the creation,
but none in even the complete accuracy of the
Gospels, or of the complete wisdom of every
word of the Epistles. The Bible to him, whatever might be its value, owed this to no supernatural origin ; and if it was greater than other
human books, it was seen to be greater only
because tried by a common standard. To him,
like all books, it naturally had its errors ; and,
like all books of antiquity, very much that is
obsolete. Creeds and dogmas he viewed in the
same spirit. None were infallible, at least in
their literal meaning, or, in that way, had for
him the least binding authority. And yet, in
spite of all this—in spite of all that science had
taken from him, he still could find in his
uninspired Evangelists, he still would find in

the fallible theorists of the Epistles, a divine clue to the way, the truth, and the life. He still could find in Christ, though dethroned from His place in heaven, a master, an example, a redeemer, a true guide to salvation. Salvation was a word which had not lost its meaning for him; he still could see a road that led to the New Jerusalem; and he still could detect on earth a veritable Christian Church, and declare that the gates of hell should never prevail against it.

A message like this, we say, was the very message that thousands were then waiting for; and the reception given the book must, to any thoughtful observer, have marked an epoch in the spiritual life of England. It revealed the existence, and it gave voice to the convictions, of a new religious body, that had been spontaneously and unconsciously forming itself. It was a body without name, or rules, or recognised test of membership. It had no organisation, it had no places of worship. But the points of agreement which united all its members, though vague in outline, were sufficiently plain in substance. Its members were all converts of science and of secular criticism. In the current sense of the word they had distinctly ceased to be Christians. But the Christian instinct was still strong in all of them; and they were longing to set on a scientific basis convictions which they thought could be secure upon no other, and which they were fully resolved they would make secure somehow. It was to these men especially that 'Ecce Homo' appealed; and to the religion which it formed, and sought to foster in them, the author has since given an extremely apposite name; he has called it Natural Christianity.

Now many people have thought, and many people still think, that Natural Christianity is to be the religion of the future; nor, whatever their opinion may be worth, are we able to call it groundless. This new religion, vague and shadowy as it seems to be, has gained in comprehension what it has lost in definiteness; and it may fairly claim amongst its professors, some of the keenest of modern intellects. It has been a moral refuge for sceptic after sceptic; and it has been of infinite comfort to them, when assailed as atheists, in enabling them to retort with a text from the New Testament It has given its own colour to Parisian Positivism; it has converted physicists into preachers of lay-sermons; and it has moved even men who repudiate all religion to profess their repudiation of it in the scriptural language of Covenanters. In our own country indeed, up to very recently, it has been almost co-extensive with ethical free-thinking. To Christians therefore of the older kind, who still believe in revelation, and in the Church's divine origin, the fortunes and the influence of this new form of Christianity cannot fail to be of very singular interest. Regarded as a popular faith, its existence has been not a long one; but it has been, in one way, strangely eventful. We propose to review the history of it during the past seventeen years, and to compare its condition at the beginning of that period, with its condition now at the end of it.

One of the chief complaints made by Natural Christianity has been that the rival system is incapable of growth. We are told, that by its supernatural postulates, it is inseparably linked to certain views of the universe which every day are being shown to be more untenable; and it cannot accept the new views that are replacing them. It may wish to do so, but it cannot. It is obliged to reply *Non possumus*. If Christianity is to live, say the Natural Christians, it can only live by growing. It must keep abreast of advancing secular knowledge, and be always ready to change or discard its dogmas, if secular criticism pronounce them false or inaccurate. Change, indeed, according to their view of the matter, is in religion the same thing as life; and Natural Christianity will reveal its living power to us largely, if not chiefly, by its constant and fearless changes. Few systems, whether of religion or government, are found to fulfil entirely the predictions of their followers or their adherents; but, at least in respect to the above matter of change, Natural Christianity has been an exception to this rule. Never was there a religion which, within an equal space of time, has changed so profoundly all its original features: or whose latter end has so rapidly forgotten its beginning. It is, as yet, hardly a generation old, and it has already not merely grown, but we may almost say that it has outgrown itself.

There are many, we do not doubt, who wil receive this last statement with indignation They will either say that notorious facts dis prove it; or else that it is incapable either o proof or disproof: or very likely they will say both. And we quite admit ourselves that we are dealing with an elusive subject, which it is difficult to treat of in very precise terms. Undue precision, however, we shall certainly not affect; nor shall we attempt to generalise further than our evidence warrants. But a piece of evidence is at the present moment before us which will enable us to speak with a certain amount of confidence. 'Ecce Homo,' as we have said already, is a work admittedly representative of the spirit of Natural Christianity, as it was in its adolescence some seventeen years ago; and we may accept its author as a representative Natural Christian. He is representative in every requisite way—in his general devoutness, in his particular moral tone, in his willingness to believe whatever science will let him believe, and in his docile disavowal of whatever it will not let him. He is representative, above all, because he is a man of exceptional intellect, and is thus quick to interpret the meaning of those scientific discoveries to which all Natural Christians are pledged to adjust their creed. We shall not be far wrong, indeed, if we regard him as a mirror in which any such Christians may see their own positions reflected. And if this be the case, the history of his opinions will be practically a history of Natural Christianity generally. For such a history he has now supplied the materials. He has given the world, during the course of the present year, a new volume, with the title of 'Natural Religion'; and by comparing the views and spirit of that, with the views and spirit of 'Ecce Homo,' we conceive we may arrive at no untrustworthy estimate, not only of the changes which the author has himself experienced, but of changes experienced also by the mass of those who share his opinions.

With regard to 'Ecce Homo,' it will be enough if we speak briefly; for the points we are concerned to notice in it are few, though of profound significance. In spite of the author's extra-ecclesiastical position, and the purely secular spirit in which he examines the phenomenon of Christianity, there are three supernatural doctrines which he never seems to have questioned, and a fourth which, if he questioned it, he questioned only to retain. The existence of a personal God, the immortality of the human soul, and some special mission deputed by God to Christ—to these three questions his scepticism seems never to have extended. The fourth question is the reality of Christ's miracles; and he decides, having gravely weighed the matter, that some, at least, of them are authentic. We beg that the reader will reflect upon these facts: he will find them full of instruction. Here are four doctrines—that a personal God exists; that the human soul is immortal; that God sent Christ to do a unique work in the world, and endowed him for this purpose with miraculous powers—here are four doctrines of the most distinctly supernatural character, and yet, seventeen years ago, the author of 'Ecce Homo' accepted them from the standpoint of Natural Christianity. We shall pause for a moment to show we are not misstating the case.

'It was the will of God,' says the author, 'to beget no second son like Christ. . . . And as, in the will of God, this unique man was elected to a unique sorrow, and holds as undisputed a sovereignty in suffering as in self-devotion, all lesser examples and lives will for ever hold a subordinate place, and serve chiefly to reflect light on the central and original

Example. In his wounds all human sorrows will hide themselves, and all human denials support themselves against his cross.'[1] This passage occurs in the closing chapter of the work; and the author proceeds to tell us, that though he is relinquishing his subject for the time being, he has by no means exhausted it. There are two points, dealt with by Christianity, which he has not yet touched upon. 'The first,' he says, 'is Physical Evil; the second is Death.... What comfort,' he continues, 'Christ gave men under these evils; how he reconciled them to nature as well as to each other, by offering them new views of the Power by which the world is governed, by his own triumph over death, and by his revelation of eternity, will be the subject of another treatise.'[2] In an earlier chapter again he writes thus: 'If we suppose that Christ really performed no miracles, and that those which are attributed to him were the product of self-deception, mixed in some proportion or other with imposture, then, no doubt, the faith of St. Paul and of St. John was an empty chimera, a mere misconception.'[3] 'Miracles,' he writes further, 'play so important

[1] 'Ecce Homo,' pp. 321, 322 [2] Pp. 322, 323. [3] P. 40.

a part in Christ's scheme that any theory which would represent them as due entirely to the imagination of his followers, or a later age, destroys the credibility of the documents, not partially but wholly, and leaves Christ a personage as mythical as Hercules. Now the present treatise aims to show that the Christ of the Gospels is not mythical.'[1]

The above extracts—and we could add to their number from almost every chapter—will be enough to inform, or else to remind the reader, how much supernaturalism remained, at the time we speak of, in this Natural Christian's creed. Indeed, so marked is this element that it may almost produce an impression that we have done wrong in calling him a Natural Christian at all. Such, however, he most undoubtedly was, as the following facts will show. We mean, when we call him a Natural Christian, that he approaches Christianity from a purely secular standpoint, and that he accepts this part

---

[1] P. 43. The writer, it is true, says presently, that for his purpose it is enough to assume the reality of the miracles 'provisionally.' But the whole tone of his volume, and many distinct expressions, show that at that time he believed in them actually; and, on the face of the matter, it is clear that his scientific conception of nature was not such as to make him think them, on *a priori* grounds, impossible.

and rejects that according to the dictates of purely secular criticism. We mean, in fact, that he disbelieves in everything that either Catholics or Protestants mean by revelation or inspiration. He does, no doubt, believe in a revelation of some sort. The most valuable of his own beliefs he believes were revealed by Christ. But he applies the word *Revelation* to the teachings of science also; and he believes that the Almighty speaks through Professor Huxley in precisely the same sense as that in which he spoke through Christ. 'Another mighty revelation,' he says, 'has been made to us, for the most part in these latter ages. We live under the blessed light of science—a light yet far from its meridian, and dispersing every day some cowardice of the human spirit. These two revelations stand side by side.' Our modern physicists, historical writers and philologists, are 'expounders,' in his words, 'of a wisdom that Moses desired in vain;' 'the least among them is greater than Moses:'[1] and, if we may add ourselves a familiar illustration of these opinions, Bishop Colenso's criticisms on the 'Books of Moses' must be a truer revelation

[1] Pp. 328, 329.

than were those books themselves. The author does, indeed, look upon the revelation made by Christ as of all revelations the greatest and most important; but the means by which we arrive at what that revelation was, are of no other kind than those by which we arrive at the history of Greece. The Christian records have, in his eyes, no special authority. He endorses some of their statements, and he rejects others. St. Mark, to him, is not more inevitably accurate than Mitford was to Lord Macaulay; nor is he more submissive to the theology of the creeds than the late Mr. Lewis was to the philosophy of Hegel. The appearance, for instance, of the Spirit in the form of a dove he at once sets aside as an evident, though harmless fable;[1] and—to come to a wider matter—the Holy Spirit itself, he declares to be really a symbolic name for 'The Enthusiasm of Humanity.'[2]

Here is a man, then, who has entirely broken away from every trammel of Christian tradition and dogmatism. He believes himself to be standing on the same intellectual ground, he conceives himself to be following the same

[1] P. 10.   [2] P. 320.

intellectual methods, as the most sceptical and atheistic of our modern physicists and historians; and, if he sees in the universe anything more than they do, he conceives that he does so simply from using their methods better. And yet this man, some seventeen years ago, could declare, in the face of all that his guides were teaching him, and appealing to no source of knowledge but such as they would recognise, that a personal God exists, that man's soul is immortal, and that Christ was miraculously deputed to lead that soul to its salvation. This man, too, was not one of the ignorant. He was a trained scholar and critic, a diligent student of the discoveries and the speculations of his epoch, and so far as intellect and moral influence went, he was evidently to be ranked amongst the foremost of his contemporaries. To minds of a certain class this will now seem hard to realise. The late Professor Clifford, for instance, during the closing years of his life, would have looked on the author's position as logically inconceivable. None the less it was his, and not his only; it was substantially the position also, as abundant evidence shows, of nearly all the earnest thinkers in England, who having discarded, at the bidding of science, the theology they had inherited from their fathers, were still imbued with the feelings, and still clung to the hopes, of which that theology till then had been the accepted explanation and analysis. In other words, Natural Religion in England was distinctly, at that time, Natural Christianity; and Natural Christianity, in the minds of even its most advanced professors, not only contained, but was actually based upon, a set of doctrines which are most unequivocally supernatural.

There were two sets of thinkers to whom this position always seemed untenable—the orthodox of all shades on the one side, and those who rejected all theism on the other. These opposing schools, though they agreed in nothing else, agreed in their estimate of this new form of Christianity. The non-theistic scientists believed firmly that the positive method could afford us no proof whatever of the existence of a personal God, and that it could afford a distinct disproof of the existence of an immortal soul; whilst, as for miracles, it made them simply inconceivable. The orthodox agreed with this estimate of the positive method so long as it was taken by itself; but, according to their philosophy of human nature, that method, though true as far as it went, was so far from being the sole road to truth, that it was the road to truth only of the least vital kind. Man had other methods of knowing, by which this was to be checked and supplemented. He had a moral sense, he had a spiritual sense, he had faith, he had a revelation. It was through these that he apprehended his nature, his destiny, and his duty; and the lower faculties employed by positive science only helped him to a true conception of things when employed together with those higher ones, and regarded as subordinate to them. Now the Natural Christians, though not disavowing the latter, reversed the position in which the orthodox school placed them. They made science the interpreter of the truths apprehended by faith, not faith the interpreter of the truths apprehended by science. This, to the orthodox thinkers and the non-theistic thinkers alike, seemed to be practically rejecting faith altogether; and the chief doctrines of Natural Christianity seemed thus to have no ground to stand upon. They seemed, indeed, to both these schools, to be simply survivals of a system which the Natural Christian had abandoned, and which the Natural Christian would soon discern to be such. The orthodox looked forward to this event as the consummation of a spiritual tragedy; the non-theistic school looked forward to it as the consummation of an intellectual enfranchisement: they both looked forward to this conclusion, whether for bad or good, as inevitable.

With this view we have always ourselves agreed. Natural Christianity, as we have said before, has numbered amongst its followers many eminent men, and, what is more than that, many noble and many excellent men. Of this fact we are perfectly well aware. The author of 'Ecce Homo' seems to us to be a marked example of it, and we fully appreciate the high qualities that are in question. But between the men and their theories we draw a sharp distinction; and our strong moral respect for the one is not at all incompatible with intellectual contempt for the other. We have always held that the theory of Natural Christianity was bound, sooner or later, to find its adherents out; that it would force on their convictions its own logical consequences; that, by the only methods which they considered valid, it would rob them of the only beliefs that they considered valuable; and that it would finally stultify, without respect of persons, the wisest and the least wise of those who had once so confidently proclaimed it. Events, it is true, have not quite answered to our expectation, but they have failed to do so in one way only—they have come to pass far sooner than we had expected. Natural Christianity is already, we believe, evaporating. The critical solvents, against which it refused to protect itself, are already doing their own legitimate work; and all the doctrines that gave it meaning or influence are disappearing in fumes at the touch of the irresistible acid. We are not speaking at random; nor, though we believe there are large numbers who will agree with every word we have said, should we have ventured to speak as we have done, without definite facts to support us. We are about to cite the author of 'Ecce Homo' himself as a witness against the very position which he did so much to render popular; and we shall show that his latest volume, alike in its arguments and its spirit, is a complete, though unconscious, condemnation of his first.

'Natural Religion' is a sad and singular book, and to any careful reader it must present itself in two lights—first, as a series of impersonal arguments; secondly, as a personal confession—a mental autobiography. We shall begin by giving a brief account of the arguments, and the ends which the author tells us he has in view in advancing them. After that we shall proceed to other considerations.

The main idea which he desires and hopes to illustrate may be gathered pretty plainly from the following sentence in his preface. 'The author,' he there says of himself, with a somewhat pointless irony, 'is one of those simpletons who believe that, alike in politics and religion, there are truths outside the region of party debate, and that these truths are more important than the contending parties will easily admit.' Now the contending parties with which he himself is concerned are not the orthodox Christians on the one hand, and the Natural Christians of former years on the other. They are distinguished far more simply. On the one hand are all men, no matter of what sect, who believe in a personal God and in man's personal immortality; and, on the other hand, all who refuse to believe in either. His contending parties, in fact, if described in our current phraseology, are the party of religion and the party of absolute atheism ; or, to use, as he does at times, words yet more significant, they are the party of faith and the party of positive science. That these two parties differ in profound and important ways he does not attempt to deny, but his contention is that these points of difference are less profound and less important than they are thought to be ; and, further, that on whatever points the two may be really opposed, there are many on which they really agree. His book, he tells us, is to be a study of these grounds of agreement.

It may probably seem at first sight to the reader that the author has set himself a somewhat hopeless task. It is nothing less, as he expressly states, than to exhibit a profound religious agreement between those who cling to religion and those who repudiate it—between theists and atheists. His contention is, however, that the words *religion* and *atheism* are used popularly in wholly inaccurate ways, and that most who call themselves atheists are not atheists at all, whilst those who call themselves the religious party have no monopoly of religion. He explains his meaning as follows.

Taking the modern man of science as a type of the so-called atheist, he maintains that this man, though he might himself be unaware of the fact, does really recognise and really worship a God; and that this God, further, is the God worshipped by the Christians. The scientific man, it is true, calls his God not God but Nature. That, however, says the author, is a mere question of words; and though words may obscure facts they cannot alter them. The Christians, he argues, believe that their God made everything, and that He is everywhere. He therefore made, and he still sustains and orders, the whole of that visible universe which we commonly call Nature. Nature, accordingly, is at least one revelation of God; and the study of Nature must, properly speaking, be at least one branch of theology. Indeed in earlier times, he observes with great justice, it was distinctly recognised as such. 'If, then,' the author continues—and he shall speak in his own words—

if, on the one hand, the study of Nature be one part of the study of God, is it not true that he who believes only in nature is a theist, and has a theology? Men slide easily from the most momentous controversies into the most contemptible logomachies. If we will look at things, and not merely at words, we shall soon see that the scientific man has a theology and a God, a most impressive theology, a most awful and glorious God. I say that man believes in a God, who feels himself in the presence of a power which is not himself and is immeasurably above himself, a power in the contemplation of which he is absorbed, in the knowledge of which he finds safety and happiness. And such now is Nature to the scientific man... The average scientific man worships just at present a more awful and, as it were, a greater deity than the average Christian.[1]

The scientific man then, says our author, is certainly not an atheist; indeed, he adds, no one can be who is not afflicted with some 'kind of mental deficiency;' that is to say, if we use the word atheism in the sense popularly given to it. In that sense, we are told, it is 'a mere speculative crotchet;' it is not a serious matter and is only skin-deep. But there is an atheism of a far profounder kind, which alone it appears may deserve the name, and which is not a speculative denial but 'a great moral disease.'

The present form (says the author), of such real atheism might be called by the general name of *wilfulness*. All human activity is a transaction with nature. It is the arrangement of a compromise between what we want on the one hand, and what nature has decreed on the other... Not to recognise anything but your own will, to fancy anything within your reach if you only will strongly enough, to acknowledge no superior power outside yourself which mus

---

[1] 'Natural Religion,' p. 19.

be considered and in some way propitiated if you would succeed in any undertaking; this is complete wilfulness, or, in other words, pure atheism.[1]

The author's meaning thus far is perhaps somewhat obscure; he therefore illustrates it by an example. One European country in especial, he thinks, has exhibited in its conduct this pure atheism he is describing. And what country does the reader think that is? He will be perhaps surprised when he learns it is not Italy, which has seized on the Papal States; it is not Germany, which has harassed the Catholic hierarchy; it is not France, which has expelled the religious orders. It is none of these; it is Poland. She, says the author, is a genuine type of 'insensate atheism. *Sedet æternumque sedebit* that unhappy Poland, not indeed extinguished but partitioned, and every thirty years decimated anew. She expiates the crime of atheistic wilfulness, the fatal pleasure of unbounded individual liberty, which rose up against the very nature of things.'

We shall not at present pause to criticise these views: we shall first, so far as we can, complete our general outline of them. We have

[2] 'Natural Religion,' pp. 27, 29.

now stated the author's first position, which once again he sums up as follows : 'Theism consists not in possessing a meritorious, or true, or consoling theory, but simply in possessing a theory of the Universe.' (P. 36.) In other words, as he reiterates with a nervous persistency, Nature, when looked at with the eyes of modern science, even if those eyes detect in it no trace either of personality or benevolence, is nevertheless in very truth God. 'Instead of atheism then', he says, 'we find the result of cancelling supernaturalism and submitting to science, is a theology in which all men, whether they consider it or not, actually do agree—that which is concerned with God in Nature.' (P. 47.)

Having thus established, as he conceives, that, in spite of all that science can take from us, it yet leaves and indeed forces on us both a theism and a theology, he proceeds to ask, how will it be with religion ? The popular instinct, he thinks, draws a 'broad distinction' between the two ; and of course if they are really separate things, that science will leave the one to us, is no proof that it will leave the other. It may have left us a theology and yet have annihilated our religion. Is this so ? That is the next question, and to it he replies as follows : 'There are two ways in which the mind apprehends any object, two sorts of knowledge which combine to make complete and satisfactory knowledge. The one may be called theoretic or scientific knowledge ; the other, practical, familiar, or imaginative knowledge ;' and applying this statement to the present question, theology, he tells us, is the scientific knowledge of God, and religion is the imaginative knowledge of Him. God, then, being the same as Nature, and theology consisting of the generalisations of the natural sciences, religion consists of these generalisations when grasped by the imagination, and through that acting on the emotions.

The author now takes a new departure, and goes on to tell us how the emotions are acted on, how science or theology is transmuted into religion. Of the results of this process, he says, there are three varieties ; and though, properly speaking, there is only one scientific theology, yet this, in passing through the prism of the imagination, reaches the moral being in the form of three religions. These are, in the first place, the Religion of Nature ; in the second, the Religion of Humanity ; in the third, the Religion of Beauty. We will take the three in order, and explain what the author means by them.

To begin, then, the word *Nature*, as the author justly observes, is unluckily somewhat ambiguous, and is only used here because there is no better available : for Nature means sometimes the All, inclusive of human nature, and sometimes the All, exclusive of it. In the present connection it is taken to mean the latter. It means a 'power not ourselves'—'a Supreme Power outside ourselves, which must be considered and in some way propitiated,' and to whose laws 'we must conform under penalties. It is, in fact, Nature in the current scientific sense. Nature, in this sense, says the author, is the object of the first of the three forms of religion ; and the religion in question consists in an emotional state of mind, in which our scientific knowledge, as it were, is held in solution. Thus we know that Nature is immense ; its law uniform ; the results of these laws various. We *feel* that the immensity is overwhelming ; the uniformity solemn and awful ; the variety inexpressibly wonderful : and such a feeling, pervading and abiding in our consciousness, is the religion of Nature.

This religion (says the author) is austere, abstract, sublime. It worships, not the individual form of Nature, but Nature itself considered as a unity. It may indeed be called out by . . . a tree, or a flower, the sky, or the sea. But in that case what it worships is as little as possible the object itself; for this religion looks through and beyond visible things : . . . loses the individual in the kind, and the kind itself in the vista of higher unities above it . . . collects them all into one grand Unity—*who* layeth the beams of his chamber in the waters, *who* maketh the clouds his chariot, and walketh upon the wings of the wind. (P. 82.)

Such then is the Religion of Nature.

The Religion of Humanity is of a more directly practical, and, as the author in one place hints, perhaps of a higher kind. Still, in one sense of the word it is a Religion of Nature also ; for man is himself an integral part of Nature—one revelation, perhaps the highest, of the all-embracing unity. What, then, is the content of this second kind of religion ? In explaining this the author finds no difficulty. The Religion of Humanity, he says, is simply the Religion of Christianity, with the supernatural part subtracted from it. It contains all the brotherly love, the willingness to spend and be spent for others, the hope, the charity, the enthusiasm, the admiration for moral excellence, that Christ taught, appealed to, and

R

awakened in the mind of the Christian world. The object of its worship is not the inhuman immensity, the inhuman order adored by the first religion. It is not the earthquake and the fire; 'it is the still small voice;' 'it is the compassion we feel for one another;' 'not the storm that threatens the sailor with death, but the life-boat and the Grace Darling that put out from shore to the rescue; not the intricate laws that confound our prudence, but the science that penetrates them, and the art that makes them subservient to our purposes.' It is in a word, all that we recognise as morally good in man; and the religion and the worship consists in our admiration and our imitation of this. Here, argues the author, is a religion with which, surely, we should be all familiar. Let us take from Christianity, as has just been said, its supernatural hopes, its supernatural sanction, and what remains is the religion just described. Nor, should anyone who has been touched by the spirit of Christianity consider that this remainder is insignificant. It is, on the contrary, by far the most important part of the whole. Indeed, the establishment of Christianity, he says, 'is in the main simply a reaction against such intolerance (*i.e.* the theological intolerance of the Jews), when the right of ideal humanity to receive worship was asserted in the heart of a people devoted to the exclusive worship of Deity.'

Lastly, we come to the Religion of Beauty. It is occasionally difficult, in the way in which the author speaks of this, to separate it from the Religion of Nature; and it is indeed bound up with it as closely as the Religion of Humanity. By putting together, however, all that we find said about it, the author's conception of it becomes sufficiently distinct and coherent. The Religion of Beauty has much in it akin to the sensuous nature-worship of the Greeks. Its spirit is indeed the spirit of that religion purified, enlarged, and rationalised by the teachings of modern science. How then does it differ from the modern Religion of Nature? It differs not so much in the object, as in the temper in which that object is dwelt upon. The Religion of Nature is concerned with the law and the unity that underlie phenomena. The Religion of Beauty is concerned with the phenomena that are the resultants of law and unity. The former, as we have seen already, worships the individual object itself

—be it a tree or a flower, the sea or the sky, as little as possible; the latter, as much. It worships not the laws that result in the primrose, but it worships the primrose itself. It sees with the eye of Art, not with the eye of Science; and yet it sees with the eye of Art after it has been purged by Science. It is in this that it differs from Hellenism. The Greek saw a fountain and a pine-tree; but it was not the gleam of the water, 'splendidior vitro,' nor the wet mossy rocks, nor the tints of the blue-grey foliage, nor the light on the bough and bark, that his emotions rested on. They passed through these to some semi-human divinities—to nymphs, or hamadryads; and the emotions due to the beauty of the things seen were wasted on the doubtful beauty of the puerile things imagined. But the Greek Religion of Nature in returning to the modern world has returned purified, and returned with an even greater, though perhaps more sober gladness. The fountain and the grove moved Wordsworth even more than they moved the poets of the Anthology. The modern worshipper sees new beauties in the water because he has no thought of any Naiad who inhabits it; he receives a deeper 'impulse from the vernal wood' than he ever could have done when the nymphs and the satyrs haunted it.

These, then, according to the present author, are the three Natural Religions which belong to man in virtue of his humanity, and of his human knowledge. They are altogether independent of the supernatural; and not only can Science never destroy them, but, on the contrary, as it grows itself, it will deepen, enlarge, and quicken them.

The author, however, is very far from being satisfied with a mere statement of the above views. Many people, possibly most religious people, will at first regard them, he thinks, as of no practical value. They will tell him that, if he likes, he may call the universe God, but that this will not make it God in any real sense of the word; and so, similarly, he may talk about his three religions, but they are not religions that will give anyone guidance or comfort, nor except by metaphor can they be called religions at all. Anticipating these attacks, he is perpetually pausing to meet them. We will consider now how he does so.

To return again, then, to the fundamental thesis of the volume, that the visible universe, as approachable by positive science, is, though it be the manifestation of no conscious or personal unity, none the less a very living God for us—the author conceives, and we think not without reason, that his average religious readers may retort much as follows upon him :—

> We know very well that the universe is glorious, but when we have said that, there is an end of the matter. We want to make atheists believe in God, and you do it, not by changing their minds, but by changing the meaning of the word God. It is not a verbal controversy that reigns between atheists and Christians; it is the great controversy of the age. Two opposite theories of the universe are in conflict. On the one side is the greatest of all affirmations, on the other the most fatal of all negations. There never yet was a controversy which was not trivial in comparison with this. It is cruel trifling to speak of compromise, it is waste of time to draw verbal distinctions. Let atheism be atheism, and *darkness keep her raven gloss*! Away with the plausible definitions which would make it impossible for any rational being ever to be an atheist! (P. 26.)

Such is the criticism of his Theistic theory which the author anticipates, and the passage just quoted is only one out of the many in which he confronts himself with the imagined objector. Let us see how he defends himself. We have already seen what is his definition of Atheism. We have now to see how he defends his definition of Theism.

In the first place, then, he says, that to be a Theist is to believe that God exists, not to believe that He is of such and such a character. Thus, Calvin was a Theist just as clearly as Canon Farrar is, though the latter believes that God will have mercy on everybody, and the former believed He would have mercy on exceedingly few. The author, however, means a great deal more than this. Not only is a belief in God *per se* independent of any belief as to his moral character, but it is independent also of any beliefs as to his 'distinctness from Nature,' or even as to ' his personality.' In short, a belief in God *per se* is simply a belief in some ' regularity in the universe to which a man must conform under penalties.' That is to say, God is Nature as discerned by the clearest vision; and Nature is God as discerned by a less clear vision. Thus far, however, he has not answered his objector; he has only put his own position in a yet more objectionable light. How can Nature, regarded merely as a regularity, take the place of God? The author answers frankly, that if by God be meant the Christian God, this God in Nature will not take his place completely; but though it takes his place only partially, it will nevertheless do so really. That is to say, Nature will not excite all the emotions that were excited by the Christian God, but it will excite a large number of emotions which Christians have always maintained could be excited by nothing except God. Therefore, says the author, even for the Christian, Nature must be God, though it be God under one aspect only. Surely, he argues, we can see this easily, we have here no occasion for moral or emotional quibbling. We need look merely at the plainest and most undoubted facts. Christians believe God to be infinite, omnipresent, omnipotent. To apply these epithets to any other Being would be blasphemy. The man of science applies exactly the same epithets to Nature, and so (with certain limitations which do not affect the case) [1] does the Christian also. Nature then, as regarded by the man of science, possesses attributes, and extorts a homage which the Christian acknowledges are proper to God alone. The Christian must therefore admit that Nature is truly God. The author constantly recurs to and dwells upon this argument, and

[1] That is to say, though the Christian may think God independent of the material universe, He is yet co-extensive with it, and He sustains the whole of it; and He is the only Being of which this can be said.

urges the validity of it by the aid of many further examples. The Christian declares God to be the sole author of his existence; the man of science declares the same thing of Nature. Of God only does the Christian say, 'in Him we live and move and have our being.' With intense conviction the man of science says this of Nature. Nature, as an historical fact, does cause such men to worship.

> Linnæus (writes the author) fell on his knees when he saw the gorse in blossom; Goethe, gazing from the Brocken, said, 'Lord, what is man that thou art mindful of him?' Kant felt the same awe in looking at the starry heaven as in considering the moral principle; Wordsworth is inspired rather amongst the mountains than amongst human beings; in solitude Byron felt the rapture that 'purified from self.' It is a paradox which will convince few, that the heavens declare no glory but that of Kepler and Newton. (P. 84.)

Here then, argues the author, are notorious instances of men who have recognised the real godhead of Nature. Nor is this recognition, he proceeds, necessarily Pantheism. It may be, and it also may not be. The Pantheist believes in an immanent cause; the ordinary Theist in a transcendent one. But these differences are secondary. They are indeed but different theories of God, based upon a common recognition of Him: just as the theory that man has a separate soul, and the theory that the soul is but the living unity of the body, are alike based on the common recognition of man. Supposing, then, what really seems to be the case, that the only Theism which science can recognise is Pantheism, we still have a God sacred and awful, an object of contemplation, of wonder, and of worship: who if we go up to heaven is there, who if we go down to hell is there also; who gives life, and who takes life away, and whose everlasting arms both in life and death are under us. Still does the Christian doubt! The author bids him turn to his Bible. That abounds, he tells him, in the 'language of Pantheism,' and 'both in Judaism and Christianity the word [God] is used for the most part in its large indeterminate sense.' (P. 88.) For some purposes—for those especially of experimental science, it will be no doubt well to retain the word Nature, but that is not because Nature is not really God, but because the name God 'is too sacred to be introduced unnecessarily; too sacred in short to be worked with.'

Such are the main points of the author's vindication of a natural and scientific theism.

That, by itself, however, he frankly admits would not, for the world at large, be a matter of great importance; and in the middle of his book, quite distinct from the chapters, he inserts, in italics, two pages of further objections:—

Has all this (he represents his critic as saying)—*has all this any practical bearing? When a religion such as Christianity loses its hold, after having possessed the minds of men for centuries, as a matter of course a sort of phantom of it will haunt the earth for a time. Its doctrines, rejected as doctrines, will be retained for a while as rhetoric and imagery; even the feelings which grow out of those doctrines will for a while survive them. A Neochristianity must inevitably arise, which will console for a short interval some feeble minds. . . . To such pious dreamers the plain English intellect loves to apply a practical test. . . It scrutinises their conduct, asks whether and in what respect they lead a different life from others who do not profess to be religious? Often* (the objector is supposed to add further)—*often this test works so effectively as to save the trouble of all further discussion. The Neochristian, who was perhaps prepared for argument, if he is not provoked by argument, gradually forgets his crotchet. He does not cease to think it true; but he ceases to find it important.*

The author devotes the whole of the latter part of his book to answering these objections. He maintains that the religion whose nature he has just been describing, is not only a real religion, but a religion with the strongest practical bearing; and he sets himself to prove this, not by a scientific forecast of the future, but by an analytic study of the present and the past. This natural Theism, he says, with the religion, or rather the three religions which appertain to it, is practically nothing new. He has said thus much already; but he must again return to the fact.

First, however, he pauses to ask what it is religion must do, to vindicate, to the popular mind, the practical character demanded of it. It must do, he says, two things. It must keep the individual in the path of right action; and it must lead him to find happiness only in right emotion. It must redeem him, that is, first from the selfish life, secondly from the sensual life. And it must do this by showing him, that such redemption is the one thing needful; that in missing it he is 'losing his own soul,' and that in that case it will profit him nothing, even should he gain the entire world. This is what most men demand of a practical religion; and this, says the author, his religion will do—this, and a great deal more besides, which most men would never demand of any religion at all.

He refers us, then, to the present and the past—to the present first. From the present, he selects the two types of men, who are supposed in general to be most free from, or most adverse to, the control of the only religion that the objectors regard as practical. These are the man of science and the artist, or the devotee of beauty. That both these men have a religion of some sort the author has already argued. He is now going to point out to us how this religion influences them. The man of science, he says, in the present state of our knowledge, considers that we have not yet a large enough inductive basis to enable us to construct any coherent moral system. The man of science therefore thinks it premature to fight for or against any of the moral systems that at present exist in the world. We must first understand, he is represented as saying, more than we do about sociology :—

But, on the other hand (his supposed argument proceeds), the laws of the universe can actually be, to an indefinite extent, unveiled; the process is going on rapidly, and infinitely more labourers are wanted to gather in the harvest. In these circumstances it is a kind of sin to occupy oneself with any other task. We have nothing to do but to think, observe, and write. And thus (continues the author), he enters upon a life to which the platitudes current about virtue have no application. . . . His pursuit stands to him in the place of friends, so that he has but few and slight ties to society. . . . But though so solitary, such a life may be to him, if not satisfying, yet preferable beyond comparison, and on the most solid grounds, to any other life he knows of. It may be full of an occupation for the thought, so inexhaustively interesting as to make *ennui*, in such a man's life, an extinct and almost fabulous form of evil; at the same time it may be full of the sense of progress made both by the individual himself, and by the race through his labours. (P. 122.)

Let us now turn to the devotees of beauty. What moral effect does their religion have upon them? The critics the author is meeting will say, 'Exceedingly little;' and the author thinks that, on the surface, they may have some ground for their opinion. For of the devotees of beauty there is one class, and that the class at the present moment most prominent, who not only seem to be indifferent to the current religious ethics, but actually opposed to them. They regard 'the pruderies of virtue as the greatest hindrance' to the proper enjoyment of life, and they side openly with 'the Medicean world against Savonarola.' (P. 121.)

Now, to the conventional moralist, it is no doubt quite true that the so-called religions of these two types of men will seem to have none of the practical effect spoken of. The man of science is untouched by the Christian moral precepts; the devotee of beauty makes a point of disobeying them. How are such men redeemed by their religion from a wholly secular life? And how, even metaphorically, can we speak of their saving their souls? The author admits that these questions are quite natural; but he has his answer to them. Neither the man of science, nor the man who worships beauty has the same conception of duty, the same conception of salvation, that is possessed by the Christian or the ordinary theist: but they have conceptions of them none the less; and none the less do they embody these in their actions. Thus the man of science finds his religion teaching him the duty of the pursuit of truth; and he patiently follows this duty every day of his life. Indeed 'he often,' says the author, 'is disposed to regard himself as not only more religious, but more virtuous than the moralist. For he believes that his love of truth is more simple, more unreserved, more entirely self-sacrificing than that of the moralist, whom he suspects onesidedly of suppressing or disguising truth for fear of weakening social institutions, or offending weak brethren.' Then, again, the devotee of beauty, though he may by a perversion of language declare himself the enemy of morality, is not so really. He is the enemy of a certain form of morality no doubt; but that is not because he thinks this to be morality, but because he thinks it to be false morality. He has a code of his own, which he thinks truer than that he cavils at, and which the author represents him as putting in the following words :—

> The man whose heart never goes forth in yearnings or in blessings towards beautiful things, before whom all forms pass and leave him as cold as before, who simply labels things and prices them for the market, but never worships or loves; of such a man we may say that he has *no soul;* and however fortunate he may be esteemed or esteem himself, he remains always essentially poor and miserable. (P. 126.)

Such are the words put into the mouth of the man who worships Beauty, merely as an avowed voluptuary; and yet even on him his religion has a redeeming influence. But the Religion of Beauty has other votaries as well, of a yet higher order. A type of these is Wordsworth. Wordsworth, says the author, was no doubt a Christian; but his Religion of Beauty stood on its own basis: to it alone was due the main characteristics of his life, and it would not have been vitally altered had Christianity never existed. We shall take occasion presently to dispute this singular judgment. The author, however, seems quite convinced of the truth of it; and therefore points to Wordsworth as the 'saint' of the Religion of Beauty. Here was a man who deliberately refused to serve either the Mammon of money or of popularity. He had his message, his prophecy to deliver to the world, and he renounced the world in order to deliver it :—

> He surrendered (says the author) the wealth that is earned by labour, trade, speculation, in exchange for the wealth that is given away. Others might purchase and hoard and set up fences, calling it property to exclude others from enjoyment. To his share fell what all may take alike. . . . the goodly universe to which he was wedded in love and holy passion. (P. 102.)

And again, speaking of such a career as this, 'This,' says the author, ' is the victory that overcometh the world.' And thus, he concludes after all, the Religion of Nature and the Religion of Beauty do both teach their votaries the same old truth, that ' man has a soul, which if he lose, it will be small profit to him to gain the whole world. . . . Neither school yield in any degree to the moralist in the emphasis with which they brand the mere worldling, or by whatever name they distinguish the man who is devoted to nothing, who has no religion and no soul, Philistine or hireling or dilettante.'

If, then, the objector can be forced to see the practical working of the Religions of Nature and of Beauty, much more easy will it be to convince him of the practical working of the Religion of Humanity. Indeed this is a point which hardly requires argument. The author seems to presume that the influence of this religion is a fact too patent to require his insisting on it; and indeed, when we consider that he identifies it with the moral side of Christianity, we think that he is justified in his presumption.

Here, then, are three Natural Religions, not only existing in spite of science, but, to a large extent, sustained and nourished by science, and actually saving souls in this so-called atheistic age. Still, says the author, there is one fact which we must not blink. These three religions not only differ, but there has hitherto been a certain antagonism between them. He is not alluding to the present only; he alludes to the past also; for these three Natural Religions, he says, have always existed, though they have enshrined themselves, in earlier ages, in forms that are now archaic. He has already said that Christianity is in reality nothing but our modern Religion of Humanity, with a certain amount of supernaturalism added to it; the Monotheism of the Jews was essentially our modern Religion of Nature; and the Greek Polytheism was essentially our modern Religion of Beauty. Now if we look back, he says, over the history of the Christian Church, we shall see that 'it has been always struggling with these [two latter] religions, and that the only peculiarity of our own age is the confident and triumphant manner in which the two enemies advance to the attack from opposite sides.' 'Thus,' the author proceeds, 'the controversy of the present day is not one between religion and irreligion, but is a controversy or a rivalry of religions amongst themselves.' (P. 128.)

Now all these three religions, he goes on to tell us, whatever their differences, are united in this—that they have one common enemy; and that enemy is irreligion. And what is irreligion? It is not any rival conviction, but it is the utter want of any conviction at all. It is 'life without worship; and the World is the collective character of those who do not worship.' The modern name for the World, he says, is 'Conventionalism.' This it is that Christ especially warred against. Even in the greatest of sinners he could find the one thing needful, if only they 'loved much :' if they had 'enthusiasm' or 'freshness of feeling.' Such persons were already more than half on his side. His only true enemies were those who had no enthusiasm; they were the world. And precisely the same spirit, he tells us, animates the three Natural Religions now. The world is their common enemy, and against that they ought to be united. They ought to be : but are they ? The author says, Not yet ; but they may be. And in such a union, it appears, lies his chief hope for the future. The three Religions are to be rivals no longer. Each is to change somewhat, and be modified by the others, until practically they become triune ; and they will thus together form a Religion greater than, at any former time, they have any of them been singly. We will proceed to describe this consummation in detail.

If three parties, who at present differ are to agree, somewhere or other there must be concessions made. Of the three parties we are here concerned with, which is to be the chief conceder? This leads us to a new aspect of the author's opinions, and one of great significance. The Religion, it seems, that is to concede most, is the Religion of Humanity, in its existing Christian form. We do not mean merely that it is to renounce its supernatural element: we suppose that already. We mean further that it is to modify its general moral tone. The author observes that certain critics have compared the Christian spirit to the spirit of old age, because both are tinged with melancholy. This view, however, he holds to be wholly wrong.

> The Christian melancholy (he says) . . . has resembled the sickliness of early youth rather than the decay of age. . . . All the faults that have ever been reasonably charged against the practical working of Christianity . . . are the faults which in the individual we recognise as the faults of youth—a melancholy view of life, in morals a disposition to think rather of purity than of justice, but principally an intolerance of all limitations either in hope or belief. (P. 153.)

Now what Christianity has to do, what it will do—in fact, what it is now in the process of doing, is to pass from this youthful stage into the healthier stage of manhood. The man differs from the youth, in having discovered that things have their limitations—that beliefs are not final, and that many ideals are unattainable. This discovery, however, is not a mere negation. It constitutes, the author tells us, a new form of religion. Having recognised how much is beyond his reach, the man realises the more keenly what is within it; and thus not only does he use his strength with more vigour, but his strength itself becomes greater, because he has ceased to unnerve himself by vague longings for the unattainable. In the place of morbid melancholy arises a healthy gladness. It is the buoyancy, the clear vision of childhood coming back to him, and asserting itself with the strength of maturity. Such a development now awaits Christianity, or has, perhaps, begun already in it. Now how will this development affect it, with regard to the two rival religions? The answer is easy. It will enable it to accept frankly the pagan delight in the sensuous beauty of life; it will enable it to recognise Art as one side of religion; it will teach it that, when rightly trained and chastened, the joy that comes to us from colour, and light, and form, and melodious sound, has nothing common or unclean in it; and that religion becomes great in proportion as it pervades humanity, not in proportion as it shrivels up into monasticism. In a similar way it will reconcile it with the great Religion of Nature. Christianity having recognised that no dogmas are final, will listen with reverence to the voice of God in Science, bidding it put aside its old supernatural theology, and take instead a theology wider still. Christianity will recognise itself as the Religion of Humanity; it will recognise Humanity as an integral part of Nature, and Nature as God—its own God for ever and ever. And thus these three religions will coalesce and form one. The Religion of Nature will be the religion at once of worship and of knowledge, of self-reverence and of docility. The Religion of Beauty will be the Religion of exalted happiness. The Religion of Humanity will be the religion of love and of progress, guided and fulfilled by the two former, and at the same time giving them their chiefest and deepest meaning.

In this way, the author thinks, religion in the future will take into itself all that is best and noblest in modern civilisation; and this reflection leads him to the final points of his argument. Thus far he has looked on Natural Religion as an influence in the life of the individual. He now proceeds to show us that it will have an influence far wider than that. Not only will it take into itself, for the benefit of each separate soul, the results of civilisation, but civilisation itself will become the same thing as religion. All the progressive nations of the world, in virtue of their knowledge and their culture, will form, through sympathy, one spiritual community —a universal visible Church, with a local habitation. The peoples of Europe, and, we presume, those of America and the Colonies also, will become that very thing which St. John meant by the New Jerusalem, and which St. Augustine meant by the City of God. Should such language seem unmeaning or fantastic, the author refers us to the Bible.

Let us consider (he writes). The Bible contains the history of a tribe that grew into a nation, of its conquest of a particular country, of the institutions which it created for itself, and of its fortunes through several centuries. Through all these centuries we hear little of heaven and hell. . . . The rewards and punishments contemplated are all purely temporal. . . . In the latter part of the book the notion of a future state first begins to appear. . . . Then in the New Testament it prevails and becomes part of the teaching of the book. But to the end of the Bible there are to be found no such heaven and hell as are put before us in Dante; the writers do not fix their attention as he does upon a future state. A few mysterious affirmations about it suffice for them. . . . This is the more to be noted, because it is characteristic of the Biblical writers both in the New and Old Testaments, that they occupy themselves especially with the future. The future is their study, but *not*—this is almost as true of the New Testament as the Old—not the future after death. It is a kind of political future that absorbs them, the fall of kingdoms and of tyrants, of Babylon, Epiphanes, Nero, and the Roman Empire, the future of Jerusalem, the expected return of Christ to reign upon the earth. . . . The idea of a future life [in the current sense of the phrase] is one that we ourselves read into the Bible; the idea which we find there, pervading it from first to last, is one which belongs altogether to practical life, and which must seem just as important to the sceptic as to the most believing supernaturalist. (P. 173.)

Such is the spirit, says the author, that we discover in the religion of the Bible; and precisely the same spirit does or will animate the religion of the modern world: indeed, little as the Christian Church has recognised the fact, the same spirit has really animated *it*. Its own greatest triumphs have been practical triumphs *here*. The first of these was the conquest to itself of the whole Roman Empire. That Empire, says the author, 'became in its turn, by the acceptance of Christianity, what ancient Israel and ancient Athens had been—a city of God.' The great event of the future is to be of a similar kind to this. A new empire, wider than the Roman, is to accept a new religion wider than Christianity. That religion is to be the triune religion of Nature, and that empire is to be the 'Universal State' of the civilised modern world. In this way, thinks the author, and in this way only, can we have any hope for the future. In this way only can there be salvation for the individual soul and stability for the State as against the forces of barbaric revolution ; and in this way the author thinks both these things will be gained. The new religion, whose nature he has been explaining to us, will more and more, he thinks, take visible form. Men will have to recognise what we have seen him urging, that 'the Church is [essentially] neither more nor less than the Spiritual City of Western Civilisation,' that it is still the salt of the earth, still a missionary and a militant body, and that a great external mission lies before it—the bringing into itself the Oriental and semi-civilised world.

The children of modern civilisation (he says) are called to follow in the footsteps of Paul, of Gregory, of Boniface, of Xavier, Eliot, and Livingstone : but they must carry not merely Christianity in its narrow clerical sense, but their whole mass of spiritual treasures to those who want them . . . the true view of the universe, the true astronomy, the true chemistry, the true physiology, to nations still lapped in mythological dreams . . . progress and free-will to fatalist nations . . . the doctrine of a rational liberty into the heart of Oriental despotisms. In doing all this . . . we shall admit the outlying world into the great civilised community, into the modern City of God.

Finally, the author says that for such a work as this there is needed an organisation, and the existing Christian Church has such an organisation ready. Now why, he asks, should not this Church or at least the Protestant part of it, recognising frankly the views that have been above stated, recognising that a Church is not based on 'exclusive dogmas,' but on the religious spirit, and that the religious spirit of this scientific age is essentially the same as the true religious spirit at all times—why should not the Protestantism of 'England and America' 'take a shape adapted to the age,' and, with all its organisation, its prestige, its traditional hold on the people, become gradually without any sharp rupture with the past, at one with this Natural Religion—this religion of the present and the future?

The reader has now before him the main argument of the volume. It remains to consider it under two aspects—its historical significance and its absolute value.

We shall gain our best insight into its historical significance by once more referring to 'Ecce Homo.' At the close of that volume the author told us that in the limits of one essay he could but half cover his subject, and he promised that by-and-by—though probably not for a considerable number of years—another volume should be given to us, in which his studies on religion would be continued. He at the same time indicated the points which this volume would deal with, and these points were as follows :—First, 'the new views' Christ gave men 'of the Power by which the world is governed ;' secondly, Christ's 'own triumph over death ;' and thirdly, 'Christ's revelation of eternity.' Half of his promise the author has now redeemed. Seventeen years have passed and that second volume has been given us ; but the other half of his promise, which related to the contents of the volume—how has he kept that? Even that he has kept to the letter, for on every one of the promised topics he dwells and dwells again ; but he dwells on them assuredly in a spirit which he then never contemplated. He said he would dwell on Christ's new views of the Father ; he does so, but only to tell us that no such Father exists. He said he would dwell on Christ's own triumph over death; he does so, but only to tell us that Christ's resurrection is a fable. He said he would dwell on Christ's revelation of eternity; he does so, but only to tell us that we are the perishing children of time.

We paused in the earlier part of this review to show how distinctly, when he wrote 'Ecce Homo,' the author reposed his faith on a supernatural basis. We must here pause likewise to justify what we have just now said, and to show how that basis has been actually now discarded by him. In the present case this is the more necessary, because there are many passages in his later volume which might seem to make this doubtful. He says, for instance, in his preface that 'the reader is cautioned not to enter on this book with the expectation of finding in it anything calculated to promote either 'orthodoxy or heterodoxy.' And he several times, in referring to supernaturalism, makes use of such phrases as '*suppose* it should finally be rejected.' It is easy to see, however, that if the present volume has any serious meaning at all, the author morally admits no '*suppose*' in the matter. The entire *raison d'être* of his arguments is that supernaturalism is, as a fact, being discarded by the world at large, and that not through any dimness of vision, or any moral obliquity; but owing to the irresistible teaching of modern science, 'under whose blessed light,' as he expressly says, 'we live;' and whose voice, it is implied in every single chapter, is for himself the unerring voice of truth. But we need not content ourselves with this indirect evidence. We have explicit statements to the same effect, which are all the more forcible because they are not specially dwelt upon, but are perpetually referred to and repeated as though they were matters of course. Thus, writing in one place, with a most delicate sympathy, of the sorrow and dejection caused by the first beginnings of doubt, he instinctively speaks of doubt as the first message of science, and he instinctively identifies science itself with truth. 'Truth (he says) in the long run cannot be resisted, and so, after whatever defence, the fortress is carried, and the phantom garrison of superstition is driven out.' Whilst, to make his meaning more unambiguous still, he repeats this same statement in a yet more trenchant form. 'To complain (he says) of the march of the scientific spirit, seems as idle as to complain of the law of gravitation itself.'

We might multiply examples of this kind of language, but for our present purpose these two will suffice. The private convictions, or the private vacillations of the author, do not affect the truth or the falsehood of the main argument of his book. Whatever he may think about the supernatural himself, for argument's sake he assumes it to be non-existent; and we have only emphasised the fact that he believes, as well as assumes it to be so, to show the singular change that in less than twenty years 'the march (as he calls it) of the scientific spirit' has produced on his spiritual life. We have already said, further, why we dwell at all on what seems to be a personal question. It is because we believe the author to be a type, as well as an individual, and because we believe that the views put forth in the present volume are representative now, as were those put forth in 'Ecce Homo' formerly. They both represent, at least so far as England is concerned, the general view of that new religious world, which has formed, or has tried to form itself, having left the old behind. 'Ecce Homo' represented it in its sanguine youth; 'Natural Religion' represents it in the death-throes that are already overtaking it.

These last words are a sufficiently plain indication of our own judgment on the arguments we have been just considering. Regarded with reference to their truth or untruth, and their practical use or uselessness, we conceive that they are based, all of them, on a profound falsehood; and that instead of giving new life to the cause in whose behalf they are urged, they show more decisively than any book we are acquainted with, how forlorn and how hopeless that cause has come to be. This judgment we shall now proceed to justify.

First, then, we must observe that our views about the volume before us are a tribute to its ability, though they are not a tribute to its truth. We consider its falsehoods to be both important and representative; but they are only important because a keen intellect has been guilty of them; and they are only representative of the present state of a cause, because they are representative of the best that that cause can do. For wide and vigorous sympathy, for delicate moral criticism, for a power of constructive imagination, and for ingenious reasoning, we consider this volume to be very remarkable indeed. So far as we know, it is the first work that has summed up, with anything like completeness, the views or feelings that, in the extra-orthodox world, are now supposed to constitute religion and theology. It is the first work, too —and this is of far more moment—that has given a formal unity to these various elements, and has presented what aspires to be the creed and the Church of the future, as anything at all approaching to a moral and a logical whole. This the present author has done, we think, successfully; nor are we by any means blind to a certain grandeur in the result. We are, on the contrary, quite prepared to admit that the natural religion, which is here offered to our consideration, not only in many ways commends itself to the mind as plausible, but impresses the imagination with a sense of its moral sublimity. Indeed, to a certain extent, it resembles the palace built by Mulciber—

> Out of the earth, whose fabric huge
> Rose like an exhalation, with the sound
> Of dulcet symphonies and voices sweet
> Built like a temple.

The magnificence of the temple we frankly and fully recognise. What we propose to show is that it is wholly without foundation; and that this is the only, or at least the principal point in which it differs from the religion whose place it is designed to take.

The author so often identifies supernatural religion with orthodox Christianity, that as we are about to speak from the stand-point of supernaturalism, it will be well to state briefly the exact ground we shall occupy. The author's arguments, though his language sometimes conceals the fact, are, as we said at the beginning, not directed against orthodox Christianity in particular, still less against any particular form of it; but rather against those two doctrines, which are common, at least in the Western world, to supernatural religions of every kind—the doctrines of a personal God, independent of the material universe, and a human soul that will survive the dissolution of the body. When we speak, therefore, in the following remarks, of orthodoxy, of Christianity, or of supernatural religion, we shall limit our meaning to these two doctrines, and we shall treat them as the only points of difference between the author and ourselves. If these once be assented to, the position of supernaturalism is gained; and further doctrines as to revelation and miracles have no longer any *à priori* impossibility.

Using, then, the word *supernatural* in the sense we have just assigned to it, we assert that all religion is supernatural that really deserves to be called religion. We will now examine the arguments that are before us to the contrary, touching firstly on those that relate to God, and secondly on those that relate to man.

The author contends, as we have seen, that if we subtract from God his personality and his independence of Nature, and conceive of Him simply as the unity of the material universe, the unity thus conceived does not cease to be God. This unity is omnipresent, omnipotent, all-embracing, all-sustaining, and so forth. In a word, for the scientific mind, it demonstrably possesses attributes which the orthodox declare can belong to none other but God. Therefore the unity of the universe is God. Now, as put by the author, this argument seems plausible; his evident earnestness lends it a kind of weight: but when we look at it on its own merits, we shall see it to be as shallow a sophism as ever imposed on anybody. We can easily test its value by applying it to a parallel question. Let us consider a corpse and let us consider a living man; and we shall find that a large part of our description of the one will coincide exactly with a large part of our description of the other. Parts of both will apply to the human body, and they will apply to nothing else. Now, when the author speaks of man in general, and argues that naturally he is a religious animal, his arguments evidently refer to the living man only, and become simple raving if referred to the dead body. If, however, his contention be sound, that Nature is really God, we can prove with equal facility that corpses are really men. If we can prove that a universe without Personality can be worshipped, we can prove that a man without personality can worship it.

So much, then, for the author's formal argument. Taken by itself it proves nothing, or less than nothing; but there are certain facts by which he points his application of it, which are far more worthy of attention than the logic they are designed to illustrate. We refer to those feelings of awe at the contemplation of the universe, of benevolence at the contemplation of humanity, and of delight at the contemplation of beauty, which certainly survive, and which seem also to be independent of, any intellectual assent to the doctrines of supernaturalism. Now we are willing to admit, quite as fully as the author does, that all this profound emotion is a part of our human nature; and that many who deny the special doctrines in question, may be far more alive to it than many others who profess them. Giving this fact, however, all possible importance, we maintain that by itself it neither leads to or constitutes anything worth calling either a theism, or a theology, or a religion. To the Christian or the supernaturalist, it presents itself as follows. Man is created by God in God's own image. He partakes of God's nature in two points especially—in his personality and in his discernment of good and evil. He has been endowed further with certain faculties by which to apprehend and respond to the love and the existence of his Creator. These are facts of human nature, just as the circulation of the blood is; and they are wholly independent of our own conscious recognition of them. We do not destroy the soul because we deny the existence of it; nor do we cease to carry the faculty of faith within us because we fail to understand, or refuse to endorse, its teachings. Thus the whole world, conceivably, might deny God, and it would still be troubled with the sense of His presence and the desire for Him. Faith would still speak, but it would speak in an unknown tongue. The traditional rendering of what it said would have been discarded, and all the alternative renderings that would be attempted would be tried by the reason, and in time found out to be nonsense. Here we may see the kind of judgment that the supernaturalist will pass on the Natural Religion described in the present volume. He will not deny that it is a fact, but he will say that it is a fact misnamed. It is not religion, but it is the embryo of religion. It bears the same relation to religion that the caterpillar bears to the butterfly or the inarticulate cry of the baby to the speech of the grown man. By being shut out from the only true expression of itself, it can only express and explain itself by a series of fatuities. It is not destroyed, but for the time it is rendered useless.

Let us speak more in detail. Man, says the

author, though he believe in no supernatural God, is conscious of awe and of admiration as he contemplates the natural universe. We grant that; but, before he proceeds further, let the author analyse these emotions he speaks about. Instead of doing this, he attempts to prove that any such analysis is wholly beside the point. Our love for a friend, he says, does not depend on our theory as to whether or no he has an immortal soul; in precisely the same way our religious admiration of the universe does not depend on our theory as to whether or no it is the work of a personal God. We are obliged to the author for offering us this analogy: let us only render it accurate, and his own position is exposed by it. Our feelings he says with regard to a man do not depend on our believing he has an immortal soul. Now let us grant that to be true, though in many cases it certainly is not; but there is one belief with regard to him which our feelings certainly do depend upon, and that is the belief that he is possessed of a personality. Supposing we were to discover that a figure we had long lived with was really nothing more than a cunningly-devised automaton—that it heard, and saw, and felt nothing—that it had no intellect, no conscience, and no affections ; it is evident that our feelings with regard to it would be altogether revolutionised. And with regard to the universe the case is just the same. The author tells us that no matter what may be our theories about it, the universe is a 'Power infinite and eternal, with which our own being is inseparably connected, in the knowledge of whose ways alone is safety and well-being, and in the contemplation of which we find a beatific vision.' And he thinks in saying this that he proves the universe, *per se*, to be God. This is the kind of language that we ask him to analyse. An analysis of it will prove a somewhat disenchanting process. In the first place, to say that we are inseparably connected with the universe is, except on supernatural grounds, an untruth or a truism. By '*we*' the author means our living and thinking selves ; but '*we*' in this sense are not inseparably connected with anything, since, according to what he calls his Natural Theology, in a very short time we shall be no longer in existence. And even while we are connected with the universe, what kind of connection is it ? A double kind, says the author. It is a connection of 'physical dependence and of spiritual communion.' Now as to physical dependence, it is no doubt a fine way of expressing it to say that in the knowledge of Nature's ways lies our only safety and well-being ; but put in accurate language, what does it really mean ? For the magnificent *Nature's ways* we shall have to write *a very few of its ways*. Of Nature's ways as a whole the wisest of us know but little : of this little only a fraction affects either our safety or our well-being, and of that fraction by far the larger part is known accurately by none but scientific men and professionals. The average human being needs but a very minute portion of it to keep him both in health and safety, and that portion is of the least impressive kind. Even the author of ' Natural Religion ' will hardly contend that a man's knowledge that mushrooms will disagree with him, or that if he gets his feet wet he will have a cold in his head, can be said to belong to the science of theology, or can convey any sense to its possessor that Nature itself is God.

The whole of the author's argument, then, with regard to the divinity of the universe, reduces itself to those vague emotions, those feelings of awe, of admiration, and of worship which are excited in us when we realise its vastness and its unity, which are said to place us in some sort of communion with it, and to make its contemplation a beatific vision for us. Now for the man who believes that the universe is the work of a personal God—a God in whose image he is himself made, who desires his worship, takes account of all his thoughts, and whom some day he trusts he may see face to face,—for such a man, such emotion has a very real significance. It is at once a purification and a prophecy. It purges his eyes so that he sees somewhat of God's glory, and it fills him with the knowledge that he will be some day in God's presence. The awe and the admiration are no doubt, full of mystery; but it is a mystery that he knows will one day be solved for him. Hence its close, its vital connection with himself. Hence the starry heavens do indeed commune with him, and the contemplation of them is a beatific vision. But the man who believes the universe to be the work of no Personality, and who believes that he has himself no other life but the present, how can he claim with the universe any such connection as this? The universe takes no heed of him; it is wholly unconscious even that he or his race exists. He may stare at the stars as much or as little as he pleases, and his health or his well-being will not be in the least affected by it. In what possible sense can such a vision be called *beatific*? It conveys to him no hint of a mystery which will one day be solved for him, and be brought into personal relations to him. If he knows little of Nature now, in a few score years he will know nothing; and, as the author often himself admits, in exact proportion as we widen our conception of Nature, the less does it seem to have any special message for us. All these fine emotions, then, of awe, of wonder, and of worship, or whatever we like to call them—the emotions at the sight and at the thought of the heavens with their countless systems, which make men catch their breath, and which bring tears to their eyes, are emotions which we may prize indeed in so far as they are pleasurable; but they are totally devoid of any rational meaning: they stand on a level no higher than the exhilaration caused by riding; and if we really set aside as a falsehood the suggestion that the Christian finds in them, they can be actually reproduced by the sight of an exciting race. We ourselves, speaking from the Christian standpoint, do not, of course, for a moment admit this to be true. The heavens declare to the Christian the glory of a personal God, and Epsom or Ascot does not ; but comparing the breathless awe that is caused by the contemplation of the firmament with the breathless suspense caused when a great race draws to its finish, the former is only higher than the latter because it contains an affirmation and an evangel that natural religion repudiates.

Let us now pass to the Religion of Beauty. With regard to this the author's position is somewhat ambiguous, or perhaps it might be more true to say that his views are somewhat confused. He says in one place that God is by no means the *only* object of religion, but only its object *par excellence*; and he seems to oscillate in his theory of Beauty between a conception of it as one aspect of God, and the conception of it as an object of worship coordinate with Him. He accordingly has here in view two classes of worshippers, one of which might be typified by Mr. Pater or by Théophile Gautier, and the other by Wordsworth.

Now those who worship Beauty after the fashion of Wordsworth are plainly supposed to worship it as one revelation of God; all therefore that we have said with regard to the worship of nature will apply equally to them. It will be well, however, to pause here for a moment, and, since the author has referred us so often to Wordsworth personally, to note briefly what his case really teaches us. The author cites it as a plain and conclusive proof of the reality of natural religion, as he himself conceives it, and of the practical effect it may have on a man's life. According to him, though Wordsworth was no doubt a Christian, and believed, as such, in the personality and the providence of God and in the immortality of the human soul, yet these beliefs were merely accidental matters; so far as Christianity had on him any appreciable effect, it was little more than a superfluous reassertion of what Nature had already revealed to him through her beauty, and was wholly independent of any of its supernatural elements. Now we believe that there are few readers of ordinary intelligence who will be for a moment deceived by this most infelicitous paradox. Since, however, the present author has stated, and laid such stress on it, we shall in passing point out its absurdity. We might easily do this by referring to Wordsworth himself, but we may spare ourselves this trouble; we need only refer to his critic. In the very page in which it is declared that Wordsworth's religion was in its essence not supernatural, it is admitted that he would have been a pessimist but for a 'Christian faith in redemption;' and we are reminded that 'he calls the doctrine of a future life "the head and mighty paramount of truths."' The author, in fact, cannot state his case without contradicting himself; and the common sense of his readers will anticipate him in the contradiction. But even were this not so, even were Wordsworth's life and views of life the results of Natural Religion, as the author says they were, they would show little with regard to that religion but its incompleteness. Apart from his genius in enforcing certain truths, the most remarkable thing about Wordsworth is the fewness of the truths that he enforced. Mr. Matthew Arnold has written with perfect justice that

> Wordsworth's eyes avert their ken
> From half our human fate :

and Mr. Ruskin, in a yet more trenchant manner, has dwelt quite recently on this same profound defect in him.[1] Whilst if we pass from his precepts to his example, we shall find that to be of a still narrower kind, and wholly useless to the vast majority of men, whose problem is, and always must be, how to face the world, and not how to retire from it.

We believe, however, when the author speaks of the Religion of Beauty, which he describes in so many words as a kind of purified paganism, that he is really conceiving of beauty, not as Wordsworth did, as one aspect of God, but as an object of worship, distinct from and co-ordinate with Him. He is at all events perpetually insisting that there can be a religion of any object that excites permanently our delight, our awe, and our admiration; and to explain his meaning, he in one place gravely informs us that America is, without any metaphor, the object of a religion to the Americans. Without, then, raising any discussion, as to beauty for the sake of beauty, or the intensity of the pleasure which our artistic nature derives

[1] Ruskin's 'Fiction, Fair and Foul—Wordsworth.'

from it, let us consider simply the broad general question, whether America, or beauty, or any object besides God, can be properly said to be the object of a religion at all.

All questions of this kind are no doubt partly verbal; but whenever more is involved in them than the settling of a terminology, what is involved in them is some distinct matter of fact. The matter of fact in the present case is as follows. Religion, says the author, is a state of feeling, the principal object of which is, no doubt, God; but God, he contends, is not its only object. Now if it is worth his while to maintain this position at all, he must mean that the feelings excited by God, and the feelings excited by the other objects he speaks of, are, as a fact, identical in their most important points. The whole question at issue is, what are these points of identity and what is their importance? The author, let us remember, is addressing himself to men who have been accustomed to identify religion with supernaturalism, and he invites them to analyse what this religion really means to them. Part of his arguments they will no doubt admit are sound. They will quite agree with him that of what they mean by religion the devil might be the object just as well as God; or a saint might be, or a dead hero might be. But this would merely mean that there may be bad religions as well as good religions, false religions as well as true; religions of one god, or of many gods, great gods or little. The devil practically would be merely an evil god, and the dead hero a little god. All these gods would be conscious, they would all be personalities, they would all take account of the conduct of their worshippers, and have the lives of them more or less in their power; and they one and all would be superhuman. Here we get to the one essential point which distinguishes religion from all other feelings. Religion is a feeling excited by some superhuman personality which takes cognizance of the human feelings excited by it. Such is the reply that could be made to the author by any one of the men to whom he is addressing himself. They would agree with him that the object of religion need not be a good god, but they would add further that it must be a god of some kind, and that there are no gods but personal gods. Other objects might excite feelings that would be like religion in some points; but they would not be

U

like it in this essential point ; and though we might very properly call them religions figuratively, they would not be religions in a scientific sense, any more than scientifically love can be called a fire, or a pair of angry eyes be said to be looking daggers.

Suppose, however, that we set this argument aside, and grant the author all that he has contended for ; suppose we grant him that there can be religions not only of bad objects as well as good, but of impersonal objects as well as personal deities, there yet remains to be made a far more important criticism. If the author's contention be not absolutely untrue, it is at all events absolutely without significance. He complains of men who were once Christians, for saying that science has destroyed religion ; and he seeks to reassure them by his long and elaborate proof that, though no doubt it really has destroyed Christianity, it has destroyed, in doing so, not religion, but only *a* religion. 'Religion *per se*' it has left wholly intact. If, however, religion *per se* need be neither good, nor true, nor useful, nor elevating, who will care to be told that religion *per se* will remain with us ? Men who think that Christianity has been destroyed, do not lament the fact because Christianity is *a* religion, but because they think it a good religion : whilst men who still believe in it, and who think it indestructible, revere religion only in so far as it leads to Christianity. Who values a system of philosophy simply because it is a system, not because he thinks it a true system ? Or who admires 'Hamlet' because it is a play, not because it is a fine play ? The author might as well comfort us, supposing all true knowledge were in danger, by urging that though in future there would be no true statements made about things, yet our children would still have statements made to them of some sort. Religion *per se* and statements *per se* are things which *per se* are equally void of meaning for us ; and the raptures of mere æstheticism would be no more a substitute for Christianity because we agreed that both they and it were religions, than Ude's Cookery would be a substitute for the Bible, because both, without doubt, were books. With regard, then, to the Religion of Beauty, the author has left æstheticism exactly where he found it. Artistic admiration is, no doubt, a source of pleasure ; and with the modification of the ascetic spirit it may, no doubt, extend itself; but to insist on calling it a religion would be, on any occasion, useless; and to drag it into the present discussion at all is worse than useless; it merely creates confusion.

We offer these remarks with all the greater confidence because, up to a certain point, the author himself agrees with us. The Religion of Beauty, if it stood alone, would be, he admits, wholly inadequate and unsatisfying; and, if it stood alone, so would be the Religion of Nature. Of this last he expressly says, that it is doubtful if it is a religion that would even justify men in living, or in bringing other men into the world. Both these Religions, that of Nature and that of Beauty, derive their chief meaning from their connection with the Religion of Humanity. The Religion of Beauty is but a gracious supplement to things of far greater value; and adorable as may be the aspect of God that we discover in nature, that aspect is dwarfed both in importance and majesty by the aspect of Him that is revealed in humanity,— 'in,' as the author puts it, 'whatever more awful forces stir within the human heart, whatever binds men in families, and orders them in states' (p. 89). There, we are told, we see God as 'the Inspirer of kings, the Revealer of laws, the Reconciler of nations, the Redeemer of labour, the Queller of tyrants, the Reformer of Churches, the Guide of the human race towards an unknown goal.' We recognise Him as the Embodiment of the 'highest' of existing things—'that is, the moral principle.' Unless we do this, says the author, unless we recognise not only that God exists, but 'that He helps us in our strivings,' and 'is not indifferent or hostile to us; we may have a theology, but we have no faith;' that is to say, we have no helpful religion. To make religion helpful, to make it worth having, to make it worth talking about, we must, the author expressly says, 'believe much and hope much,' without regard to the future of humanity. We must not only believe that the moral principle exists, but we must believe that its power will grow and become supreme; that it is not only the highest of principles, but the strongest also, and that it will guide the human race to some noble state of existence, equal, if not superior, to all our loftiest visions.

Otherwise (says the author), if reality, when we acquire

the power of distinguishing it, turns out to be not merely different from what we expect, but much below what we expect; if this universe, so vast and glorious in itself, proves in relation to our desires narrow and ill-furnished, . . . then humanity [like the doomed and perishing individual] has its necessary old age; and if its old age, then surely that which lies beyond old age. . . . We must abandon ourselves to pessimism (p. 155). . . . All human griefs alike [will] seem little worth assuaging, human happiness at the best too paltry to be worth increasing. . . . Life [will] become the more intolerable the more we know and discover, so long as everything widens and deepens except our own duration, and that remains as pitiful as ever. . . . What would Natural Religion avail then?[1]

Here we arrive at the foundation of the author's teaching. All the arguments he urges in the whole of this volume depend for their meaning on this one belief, that the future history of our race will be one of unceasing progress; and by progress he means certain very distinct things. He means diffusion of political liberty, diffusion of the material luxuries of life, the fraternisation of nations, the abolition of war, and so on. But this is not all he means, nor is it the most important part. This is the body of progress merely, it is not its soul. The soul of progress is the

[1] P. 262, where the author explains at length what he means by pessimism.

diffusion and the development of the spiritual riches of our nature—of our joy in art and in beauty, of our awe at the majesty of the universe ; but principally of our love for our fellows, our readiness for self-sacrifice, our recognition of the inherent worth of life, and above all of the sacredness of our own higher natures, on which depends our recognition of the sacredness of ideal humanity. To believe that life, and the conditions of life, will, in the above sense. for ever go on progressing till they can progress no longer, and that after that they will never retrograde -- this, says the author, and this alone is 'faith'; this, and this alone, makes religion valuable, or gives the smallest meaning to all the hopes which he is so earnestly holding out both to himself and those he addresses.

We might pause here, were it worth while to do so, to show that Natural Religion, as described in this volume, is simply the positivism we have so long been familiar with, only changed in so far as the culture of the author has filled in its outlines, and his Christian phraseology confused them. We will leave the reader, however, to consider that point for himself, and pass on to one of far greater importance. Supernaturalism, says the author, has failed, because it has founded itself upon dogmas, and made religion dependent on an assent to them. Dogmas, he says, are always liable to modification or disproof; and supernatural dogmas are never capable of proof. Thus supernaturalism for many men has put all religion in danger, by resting it on a weak foundation, and a foundation that does not belong to it. Religion really, he says, has nothing to do with dogmas, nor is a Church like 'a philosophical school, held together by doctrines. . . . It is more like a state than a school. . . . Imagine a state resting upon dogma!' 'The *truth* of a religion,' he adds, 'is a phrase without meaning. You may speak of the truth of a philosophy, of a theory, of a proposition, but not of a religion, which is a condition of the feelings' (p. 222). Therefore, he argues, religion is indestructible; and not religion only, but a helpful, a saving religion, which shall open to humanity and every member of it for ever, a treasure compared with which 'the whole world' is as nothing. Such is the religion that he has been describing in this volume; and such a religion, he says, is independent of dogmas.

Now of all forms of misleading and empty cant, the popular modern cant against dogma, as such, is perhaps the most misleading and emptiest. To say this, however, is one thing, and to prove it another; and the proof, in some cases, may be long, though never difficult. The present author, however, saves us all trouble in the matter, and supplies us out of his own mouth with the materials for his own confutation. In the very act of declaring that religion does not rest upon dogmas, he is giving us nothing but a practical proof that it does. He makes a clean sweep of the accepted dogmas of supernaturalism, but he only destroys these to put another dogma in the place of them. His own Natural Religion is itself founded on a dogma, as much as was ever any system of Christianity; and little as he seems to perceive what he is doing, he not only admits the fact, but is perpetually insisting on it. For what is a dogma? It may be defined in three ways. In the first place, it is a proposition as distinguished from an emotion; in the second place, it is a religious proposition as distinguished from other propositions; and in the third place it is a proposition, which, though evidence *may* support it, must be assented to as well upon grounds deeper than evidence; it must be assented to by faith. Now what have we just seen? Have we not just seen that, by the author's own showing, his whole Natural Religion depends for its whole value on our assent to one cardinal proposition, which is stated by him in various ways? We have dwelt upon it only a moment ago; but let us now repeat it. One way of putting it, as we saw, is as follows—'This universe, so vast and glorious in itself, is, in relation to our own hopes for the future, not narrow or ill-furnished.' Another way is as follows—'Humanity is growing out of its youth into its healthful manhood, and that manhood will never decline into old age.' And again, another way is as follows—'The omnipotent and omnipresent power embodied in the universe, helps us in our strivings, and is not indifferent or hostile to us.' Now how, we ask, does this proposition differ in any essential way from the various dogmas on which Scriptural religions base themselves? It is a proposition, it is not an emotion. It is, further, a religious proposition; and it is, further, as the author takes special pains to emphasise, not to be held at the precarious mercy of evidence, but is to be assented to as a certainty, by an act of *faith*. Of course it may be true, in the stricter sense of the word, to say that religion is a state of the feelings; but these feelings, as the author himself shows us, depend on a certain judgment with regard to the object of them, which can only be expressed or thought in the form of a dogma or proposition. Our emotion with regard to the universe depends on our judgment with regard to the universe; or in other words, our religion depends upon our dogma. If we cling to our dogma as true our religion will remain with us; if we reject our dogma as false our religion will leave us. For this reason, in common language, we are accustomed, and very properly, to speak of a religion being true: and to declare, in this connection, that such language implies a falsehood, is neither more nor less than a miserable quibble. One man respects another because he believes him honest. If he finds him out to be a rogue he will cease to respect him. Everyone knows that the respect is not the belief; but everyone knows that it is based upon it. If anyone takes the trouble to tell us that respect is not a proposition, but a state of the feelings, we shall merely think that he is saying what is superfluous; but if he argues from this that the feelings do not depend on our assent to the proposition, we shall merely think that he is talking nonsense. And the same is the case with religion. The common sense of the world has always perceived this truth; and the present author, in his laborious effort to combat it, has simply succeeded in giving the most signal proof of it that it is possible to find in the religious literature of the century.

Now comes a further question. Since Natural Religion is, after all, thus based upon a dogma, what grounds have we for endorsing that dogma as true? That is to say, what grounds have we for any certitude as to the continuous progress and glorious future of humanity? It is not our province here to discuss on its own merits this much-vexed question. We shall merely confine ourselves to the author's own treatment of it, and that certainly is full of a strange significance. Not once in the course of this whole volume does he make any attempt worth speaking of to show any grounds for the faith that he requires to be in us. On the contrary, he rarely makes any direct allusion to it, except to suggest darkly that it may have no grounds at all. 'Apart from pessimism,' he says in one place, 'there is nothing to prevent us from worshipping.' But he seems to wince at the very sound of the word *pessimism*, and he sharply drops the question. Such is his conduct generally whenever he is face to face with it. Often, however, it is glanced at obliquely by him, and then he deals with it somewhat more in detail, but with what result? Always to hint, not that the progress of the human race and its religion is certain, but that it is beset by dangers and uncertainties. Whilst he is enlarging on the delights of what he calls 'the higher life,' he admits the difficulty of recommending these delights to the multitude, and he admits that the lower life may bring most complete content with it; and whilst he enlarges on the mission of our existing Western civilisation, he hints broadly that in the course of a few generations the whole of that civilisation may be destroyed by a social revolution. Nowhere does he offer us any tangible foundation for the faith that is to remove these mountains of doubt or of despondency.

We do not blame the author. The defect is not in him, but in the hopeless and irrational cause of which he has made himself the champion. All his fellow-champions are in like case with him. There is one foe which they cannot face, and that foe is pessimism. Neither Comte, nor George Eliot, nor Mr. Herbert Spencer, are more convincing on this point than is the present author. Not one of them can confute the argument of the pessimist. Instead, they, some of them, drown it in uproarious denial; some of them try to smile as though they had never heard it; and some of them, unintentionally, are forced to admit its truth.

Of this last class is the author of 'Natural Religion,' and we propose to conclude our criticisms on his system, by adding certain of his own, which are yet more severe than ours. Having shown already that he has failed to convince us, we shall proceed to show that he has failed to convince himself.

In the first place, then, we may remark that throughout the whole volume the tone is one, not of enthusiasm, but rather of a forlorn patience. The author seems to be a man who is still searching for the pearl of price after he has secretly given up all hope of finding it. His heart is still with the Christianity which he has repudiated. In the natural world he has entered he is an exile by the waters of Babylon, and he is trying in vain to sing the Lord's song in a strange land. He tries to call the heathen city Jerusalem, but in his heart he finds it only a Zion of bitterness. We do not, however, refer to his general tone merely; we refer also to his own explicit statements. The reader shall hear a few of them. The highest worship, he says, is not reached until 'passing by an act of faith beyond all that we can know, we attribute all the perfections of ideal humanity to the Power that made and sustains the universe' (p. 168). And again, in another place, he admits yet more plainly that he 'can conceive no religion as satisfactory that falls short of Christianity' (p. 25). Admissions of this kind—which seem like involuntary *asides*—are scattered throughout the volume; but there is no need to cite more of them, since the sum and substance of all of them is gathered up, concentrated and emphasised, in the three concluding pages.

These pages, as related to the rest of the volume, form the most curious conclusion to any series of arguments that we ever remember to have met with. They form a section by themselves, added as a sort of postscript; and the gist of them is a flat contradiction of everything that their author has been just contending for. 'Throughout this volume,' he says, at the beginning of this section, '... we have denied that supernaturalism is necessary either to the idea, or to the practical vigour, or to the popular diffusion of religion' (p. 258). And this is perfectly true; it is exactly what the author has done. But let us turn over a single page and what shall we find there? We shall find the author, after two brief paragraphs asking if that very supernaturalism which he has been thus setting aside 'may not be precious, nay, perhaps indispensable' (p. 259) as a 'supplement' to his 'Naturalism.' Nor does he leave the question in any ambiguous state. 'No sooner,' he says, 'do we try to think that the known and the natural ... can suffice for human life, than Pessimism raises its head.' And then the author proceeds in a passage some words of which we have already quoted:—

The more our thoughts widen and deepen, as the universe grows upon us, and we become accustomed to boundless space and time, the more petrifying is the contrast of our own insignificance. . . . A moral paralysis creeps upon us. For a while we comfort ourselves with the notion of self-sacrifice; we say, what matter if I pass, let me think of others. But the *others* now become contemptible to us no less than self; all human griefs alike seem little worth assuaging, human happiness too paltry at the best to be worth increasing. The whole moral world is reduced to a point; the spiritual city, the 'goal of all the saints,' dwindles to 'the least of little stars.' Good and evil, right and wrong, become infinitesimal, ephemeral matters, whilst eternity and infinity remain attributes of that only which is outside morality. The affections die away in a world where everything good and enduring is cold; they die of their own conscious feebleness and bootlessness. 'Supernatural religion,' adds the author, 'met this want by connecting love and righteousness with eternity. And if that is shaken,' he proceeds with extreme pertinence, 'what would natural religion avail then?' (P. 262.)

That is precisely the question that we ourselves have been asking, and we are pleased to perceive that at the close of his volume the author's real answer exactly coincides with our own; and that answer is 'Nothing.' 'Natural Religion' is a sad and singular book. It is sad as a picture of an earnest mind caught in an intellectual tangle from which it is unable to free itself; it is singular as being the work of a trained and subtle reasoner, and yet ending with

X

a formal repudiation of the proposition it was written to vindicate. We have said the latter end of Natural Christianity has in seventeen years forgotten its beginning. The author of 'Natural Religion' has done the same in a fewer number of chapters.

ATHEISTIC METHODISM, OR THE BEAUTY OF HOLINESS.

A Reply to Critics.

The various writings in which I have discussed the value of life, in especial my volume 'Is Life Worth Living?' have been made the subjects of so much vindictive criticism, that I have been often urged to make some reply in defence of them ; and certain incidents which have occurred quite recently, have combined to offer me a convenient opportunity for doing so. In the first place, since the publication of these writings of mine that are in question, a work has appeared by one of the most eminent thinkers of the time, which, though in no way designed to be a special attack upon myself, has yet turned out to be so practically. I refer to Mr. Herbert Spencer's 'Data of Ethics,' which the author implies and his disciples believe to be a final and formal statement of the new philosophy of life. Secondly, there has appeared in America, from the pen of these very disciples, an entire volume,[1] in which, passage by passage, I am angrily and laboriously refuted, with Mr. Spencer's weapons, and from Mr. Spencer's philosophical stand-point; and, lastly, in England, a fluent and intellectual lady, Miss L. S. Bevington, writing, so report says, under Mr. Spencer's personal direction, has devoted two essays[2] in 'The Nineteenth Century' to applying the arguments urged in 'The Data of Ethics' to mine. Considering therefore Mr. Spencer's high repute, and how he has organised the scattered speculations of our non-theistic thinkers, such criticisms as those I have just alluded to have seemed to me to deserve my best attention.

My best attention has been given them, and not without result. They have strengthened my belief in all I have urged hitherto, and in the ultimate helplessness of all that can be urged against it. But though my critics have not convinced me that my argument itself has any flaw in it, they have shown me certain defects in my own way of stating it, which I am anxious at

---

[1] *The Value of Life: A Reply.* New York. Putnam's Sons.

[2] *Modern Atheism and Mr. Mallock.* By L. S. Bevington. *Nineteenth Century*, October and December, 1879.

the same time to point out and to remedy: and the criticisms in question, especially those of Miss Bevington in 'The Nineteenth Century' have taken a shape which makes the task a very easy one.

To begin, then, with this lady, her state of mind as regards myself seems, if somewhat singular, to be also typical and instructive: for not only it seems have I roused her intellectual powers against me, but in a still greater measure her moral indignation also. She proclaims herself lost in wonder as to what conceivable 'cause, social, moral or religious, I could expect to serve by arguing in the way I have done.' No conceivable good, so far as she can see, could come of it: and my only possible motive, as she strongly hints, must be either a degraded or perverse one. Others, perhaps, may also think as she does—indeed, my censor in America is even more severe than she is—and it may therefore be well briefly to say a word or two on the matter. To me the answer to the question seems sufficiently obvious: indeed, my critic has herself given a part of it. My arguments, she confesses, are of value to all scientific writers, who would know at what points in morals men were asking for 'definite scientific utterance.'

Surely one would think that this was no superfluous task, to browbeat the reluctant oracle, by whose responses we are told that the whole world is to guide itself, and to force its lips to utter some definite and coherent sentence. And the task would be of equal use, whether its aim were to make the oracle help us or to make it reveal its helplessness. Surely here is a motive that one would think is plain and sane enough. And is it not equally plain that there may be yet another also, springing out of and completing this one? What good, exclaims my critic, can I think to gain by elaborate attempts at reducing unbelievers to despondency, and at loosing their hold upon hopes which they are still struggling to cling to? The answer is near to hand. For those who hold that on theism the hopes of the human race depend, and that this alone can sustain it in the trial or transformation to which it seems about to be subjected, it may be of the utmost moment to strip from the unredeeming philosophies all the fragments of truth which for a moment disguise their nakedness; and to show, though at the cost of pain and despair to many, that the end of these things is death. Whenever a fight grows hard between a false belief and a true one, there will be found worthy soldiers fighting on either side; and the iron will go through the souls of many who, so far as we can see, have little deserved to feel it. But such pain in the present case does not seem needless. To the eyes of the believer, a large and leading body of men are entering an Inferno which they honestly mistake for paradise. At present they are only on the confines of the 'brown air;' and they trust that it will grow brighter as they dive further into it. To call them back by the way they have gone seems hopeless. The one course is to plunge them as quickly as may be to the lowest circle, where the God they have denied is most completely absent; that so at last they may emerge on the other side, and again see the stars.

And now having said this, let me proceed to what lies before us—to the special points that I am about to deal with now. The main questions that my late volume has treated have been, roughly speaking, two: first, the relation of human life to theism; secondly, the relation of theism to exact knowledge and thought. It is the former of these only that my fair critic in 'The Nineteenth Century' has touched upon; and what

I am about to say will accordingly be confined to that. Let us define more closely the exact scope of the argument. It is concerned with the truth or falsehood of two statements of my own, which my two critics, English and American, have, for precisely the same reasons, formally contradicted. I have maintained that theism, with its attendant doctrine of man's personal immortality, 'has a practical effect upon practical life—upon what men do, and what they forbear to do—what they think of themselves, and of one another.' Without these beliefs, I have said further, 'there can be no standard by which the quality of pleasure can be tested; that truth as truth, and virtue as virtue, cease to be in any way admirable.' And should these beliefs ever quite vanish from the world, I have predicted a catastrophe as the result, that might be not unfitly spoken of as the second fall of man. My critics maintain, on the contrary, that not even in its most modified form is such a catastrophe possible. That a vast change is imminent they indeed admit readily, but it is a change, they say, that does not touch virtue, nor any of the great emotions that are at present connected with it. There is, they assure us, to be no lowering of life; our highest hopes and pleasures, and all our profoundest consolations, are to still remain to us; and 'so long as man is man,' says Miss Bevington, 'virtue, as *virtue*, will never cease to be admirable.'

Such are the counter-statements that I am again about to deal with, and which I trust to end by setting in a far plainer light. Here and there, perhaps, I shall have for a moment to repeat myself; but I agree with Mr. Herbert Spencer in not much regretting this. 'For only,' as that writer says, 'by varied iteration can alien conceptions be forced upon reluctant minds.'

What I have to do chiefly, however, is not to repeat, but to correct myself. In parts of my former writings there has been a certain ambiguity, with which both my critics have very justly taxed me. It lies in my use of the two words *virtue* and *morality*, which on certain occasions I have seemed to confound with happiness; and, indeed, in the cases I am referring to, they practically were inseparable. In thought, however, at any rate, they are always distinct things; and we shall save much confusion if we transfer this distinction to language, and resolve always to retain it there.

Let us begin with this: and we cannot do better here than refer to the positive writers themselves. Mr. Herbert Spencer shall speak first. 'No school,' he says in his latest volume, 'can avoid taking for the ultimate moral aim a desirable state of feeling called by whatever name —gratification, enjoyment, happiness. Pleasure, somewhere, at some time, to some being or beings, is an inexpugnable element of the conception. It is as much a necessary form of moral intuition as space is a necessary form of intellectual intuition.'[1] And 'if,' he says further, 'we call *good* the conduct conducive to life, we can only do so with the implication that it is conducive to a balance of pleasures over pains.'[2] Morality, or goodness itself, says my American critic, repeating my own words, 'is not the prize of life.' That prize is happiness; and 'morality,' he says, 'only furnishes the negative conditions.'[3] Miss Bevington is even more explicit. 'Every one else,' she says, 'knows and affirms, and no positive moralist attempts to deny, that virtuous conduct is only to be achieved at all for the sake of what lies

---

[1] *Data of Ethics*, p. 46. [2] *Ibid.* p. 45.
[3] *The Value of Life*, p. 229.

beyond it.'[1] And, finally, I may add to this a former remark of my own, that all those actions which my critics praise as virtuous, are only the 'creatures' of the happiness they lead to, 'and can have no more honour than the latter is able to bestow upon them.'[2]

What follows then is this, and all our positive writers will do well to remember it. The entire worth of life—the dignity, the glory, or whatever we please to call it, of humanity—rests on the fact that humanity is capable, not of virtue, or of heroism, not of truth, or purity; but that it is capable of pleasure, of gratification, of enjoyment, or of happiness. The former are of value only because they lead to the latter, at some time, and for some certain persons; and we only praise or felicitate those pursuing them, in so far as the gratification they lead to has been in some way tasted by themselves. Thus all our interest in humanity, and all our ardour in behalf of it, must rise and fall with the fortunes of one belief—our belief that humanity does secure, or that it some day will secure, a preponderance of

---

[1] *Nineteenth Century*, October 1879, p. 598.
[2] *Is Life Worth Living?* p. 57.

pleasurable over painful feelings; or, in other words, that certain human brains shall at all events some day, and perhaps do now, exist in a certain state. The one and only thing in the universe that, according to the positive system, can *per se* be adored or valued, is, as Mr. Spencer expresses it, 'the balance of pleasures over pains'—the aggregate of agreeable states of consciousness that shall be ours between our births and death-beds.

Now all this, with but a single difference, the theist admits quite as fully as any one; and indeed so far as it goes it can be denied by no sane person. Of the difference in question we shall come to speak presently; but there is another point that we must first go on to deal with. We must first ask how, since the ultimate aim of action is nothing but unalloyed gratification, not gratification but virtue is the foremost thing that the positive teachers commend to us. The answer, of course, is easy; but none the less will it be well to restate it clearly. It lies in the fact that we are, as Miss Bevington expresses it, 'all helplessly social.' In other words, we each need some help or some self-restraint from others; we each owe others some help or some self-restraint in return; and it is on the gradual adjustment of these mutual offices that all human progress depends. It is the voluntary rendering of such help, or the voluntary practice of such self-restraint, that is called by the positivists indifferently virtue, righteousness, or morality. Now the acts that these names are applied to are all of them, in their primary nature, an unmixed pain to us. They are the foregoing of what is directly pleasing to ourselves, that others may obtain what is directly pleasing to them; and as such, though the laws could of course in some measure enforce them, it is a psychological impossibility that they would ever be voluntary—sought, that is, for their own sake, as a gratification. To be voluntary, or, in other words, to be virtuous, these painful acts must become flavoured with a taste of pleasure for the agent—with, as Mr. Spencer would say, 'some state of feeling that is desirable.' And there is in all of us a certain natural sense, by which such pleasure can, within limits, be given. This sense is the sense of sympathy, our possession of which not enables only, but, within limits, compels us, to rejoice and suffer with others, as well as with ourselves; and makes their welfare in some degree traverse our own. It is this sense of sympathy, and this alone, that, for the positive thinker, makes virtue possible. It alone consecrates the beggarly elements of our own pain, changing the substance of it although it leaves the accidents, and makes us partakers sacramentally of the agreeable feelings of our neighbours, and even of our remote posterity.

It will be seen that, thus analysed, a virtuous act is this. It is an act whose necessary concomitants are two distinct feelings, a feeling of personal pain, and a feeling of vicarious pleasure that outweighs it. Each of these two is equally necessary. Without the first, the act would not be virtuous; without the second, it would not be possible. But yet more is implied than this. In producing the clear balance of vicarious pleasure, in securing its final victory over personal pain, it is understood always that there is a struggle, never easy, and in some cases desperate; and the one end and object of all moral systems is neither more nor less than to succour and guide the combatant. When the triumph is won, says Miss Bevington, it is a triumph of '*will*';

'*will*,' she says, ' and I use the word advisedly.' We may therefore define the virtue, the morality, or the righteousness with which we have to deal in the two following ways. It may be defined, by the analytical spectator, as the will, when it so intensifies sympathy that the pain an act gives to self is more than neutralised by the pleasure it gives to others. It may be defined, by the virtuous agent, as personal pain, overbalanced by vicarious pleasure. Such is the definition of it in its completeness. But viewed as a thing to be desired and striven for by the agent—viewed in the only light that can make its attainment possible—the definition will be yet shorter. We must define it only as the balance of vicarious pleasure, without any account being taken of its near connection with pain.

I will now check this account of the matter by reference to the critic to whom for the present I am more specially adverting. Virtue, from the positive thinker's stand-point, is defined formally by Miss Bevington as 'such conduct in another as forwards his own interests at that other's cost;' and she adds further, as a second ground for praising it, that it is not thus good in its outward effects only, but it is also 'a good achieved with difficulty.'[1] She is here in entire agreement with Mr. Herbert Spencer; it will be plain, therefore, that I am not misleading the reader.

Now that virtue, thus regarded, is a good when tested externally, may doubtless be true enough. But this theory of it does but take us a very short part of our way. 'It is,' as Miss Bevington herself truly says, 'null and void even as a theory, unless it can be married to existing human emotion, and can so sway the motives which underlie conduct.' In other words, the first practical task of the moralist is not to present virtue as agreeable to others—that for the present we may take for granted—but to present it as an end for personal action; that is, as an end agreeable in some way to ourselves. Virtue to be virtue, must be followed voluntarily—nay, with ardour; and an agreeable feeling of some kind is, therefore, in Mr. Spencer's words, 'an inexpugnable element in our conception of it.' There must, if I may borrow his phraseology yet further, be 'a particular mode of (agreeable) feeling, temporarily existing as a concomitant of each kind of beneficent action;' or the benefi-

[1] *Nineteenth Century*, October 1879, p. 591.

cent actions would never be done at all. It is only such feeling that, in the absence of outward force, can make any action possible. Nor does it matter that the pleasure the virtuous act produces may pass in its course through others. The important point is that like an electric current, no matter how long the circuit, it returns without fail to ourselves. Virtue, therefore, for the practical, for the preaching moralist, is neither more nor less than a particular mode of pleasure, for which he has to cultivate a taste amongst disciples professedly reluctant. That the rudiments of the taste exist is admitted by all; but the reluctance to have these developed is admitted also—indeed, not admitted only, but, as we have seen, emphasised as essential by the positive thinkers themselves. Enormous difficulties stand in the way of our conquering it —difficulties so great that the whole history of mankind hitherto has been little else but an ever-baffled struggle against them.

This struggle, which religion has sustained so painfully, our new philosophers tell us they will undertake with a better heart; and this for two different reasons. One is that the course of human events, independent of any conscious effort on our part, tends of itself to evolve that general happiness which it is the essence of virtue to aim at consciously. Such a theory, however, taken by itself, is rather a sedative to virtue than a stimulant; and the moralist, as a moralist, has nothing at all to do with it, unless he can 'marry it,' in Miss Bevington's language, to a quite other set of considerations. It is nothing to him that, whether we will or no, there are certain impersonal forces that are inexorably moving all of us in one direction. The thing precious in his eyes is that with these forces the will of each of us should co-operate. It is his one task to induce the will to do so; and the task, he admits himself, is a very hard one. Still the positive thinker maintains that it is no harder for him than for the religious thinker; indeed, in some ways easier. It is with his reasons for this confidence—not with his theories, however true, about the tendency of impersonal forces—that we first of all have to deal.

Let us inquire, then, what this confidence means. It means a confidence that he can do some particular thing. But what? It can be defined very narrowly. We have seen that his general task is so to present virtue that the will shall seize on it always as the chief end of action: and he must present it, for this end, as essentially a balance of pleasure outweighing a load of pain. It is on the character of this balance, as related to the virtuous agent, that the whole question hangs; and the power of the positive moralist, and the entire meaning of his system, are determined by how he handles it.

The task before him is indeed formidable. What he must prove, and what he engages he will prove, is that this balance of pleasure is, for the agent himself, of all pleasures the intensest—that it is, for him subjectively, the most agreeable of all sensations; so agreeable indeed, that all others, matched with it, are, as George Eliot expresses it, 'dross for ever,' and that in so far as he fails to secure it, he really has nothing although he possesses all things. That I do not exaggerate the sentiments which my critics engage to justify, can be shown by extracts from the words of Miss Bevington herself. That lady shows a nervous zeal in proclaiming that 'every word' I have said on this head 'is emphatically true'.[1] She speaks of virtue as 'that thing we love so well . . . and which we

---

[1] *Nineteenth Century*, October 1879, p. 587.

hug as our choicest treasure.'[1] 'It would be a terrible thing,' she says, 'to be equally happy, and equally prosperous, supposing such a case were possible, without a *belief* in right and wrong *as such*;'[2] and the results that would follow the destruction of this belief would be, she says, 'thoroughly dismal and sickening.'[3]

Nor is this unique intensity of the pleasures brought by virtue ascribed to them, by the positivists, through any kind of bravado. They are obliged to ascribe it. Their system makes them do so, as we can soon readily see.

We will illustrate the whole case by a short and homely parable. Bill and James, we will say, are two tourists, whose keenest personal pleasure is in cutting their own names on the roofs of public buildings. They take a long and toilsome walk, that they may perform this feat on the highest pinnacle of a certain cathedral tower. Having climbed at last, however, to the lofty scene of action, they find, to their horror, that they have only two minutes to spare, that the leads of the coveted pinnacle

---

[1] *Nineteenth Century*, October 1879, p. 602.
[2] *Ibid.* p. 587. The italics are in the original.
[3] *Ibid.* p. 586.

are some distance out of reach, and that if either is to cut his name at all, it can only be one of them raised on the other's shoulders. There is, for a moment, a struggle in the minds of both. Then Bill's will triumphs, and lifting James up, who cuts his name in rapture, Bill's only pleasure, the only reward of his walk, is such of James's pleasure as, received by himself vicariously, is in excess of the pain consequent on his own self-denial.

Now, in this short drama, of which Bill is the moral hero, we have all the elements of virtue, as conceived of by the positivist, in their immediate bearing on the agent. We see what is virtue, we see what is not virtue, and we see that which, while resembling it, yet is not it. The delight of the two tourists in cutting their respective names stands here for the logical end of life, and the vindication of it as being worth the living. But the separate pursuance of this end by each of them is not virtue; neither is the suffering undergone by each in his long and toilsome walk. This last, as Miss Bevington puts it, is 'but disguised personal expediency;' and so far from being identical with virtue, is, in her opinion, in strong contrast to it. We find virtue only in one place; that is, in the foregoing by Bill personally of the one end of his existence, and choosing instead, as it were, only such a margin of it as, conveyed to him at second hand, is not eclipsed by the pain of his own personal loss of it.

Or let us have recourse to yet another parable; and compare the gladness of life to some splendid opera, which all the musical world is thronging eagerly to hear. Were there enough seats to accommodate all the applicants there would indeed be unmixed pleasure; but there would be no pleasure that could be praised as virtuous. Virtue arises only through the theatre being too small for the audience, and through me, for instance, resigning willingly a seat already reserved for me. I am not virtuous in this case because I drive to the theatre in a draughty hansom. I am not virtuous because I fully enjoy the opera. I am virtuous only in so far as I enjoy nothing of what I came to enjoy, but am yet happier than if I had done so, because I know my friend is enjoying it; though I may myself be catching my death of cold in the passage, and hear no more classical music than the barmaids' voices in the refreshment room. I say I am virtuous only because I get my enjoyment thus, and under these conditions—because the indirect end of life, largely deadened by pain, is more agreeable to me—to me personally—than the direct one ever could be, even with no pain to detract from it.

Let us consider well these two parables : for they are all the more instructive because in their details they are so trivial. The severe moralist may say that my pleasure in the opera is only a selfish luxury; and that the tourist's pleasure in cutting his own name is only an offensive vulgarity. But yet when we each of us, respectively, secure these ends for others, and, at the expense of pain, get the despised pleasures at second hand, these despised pleasures are held to change their character, and they become the one thing in life we are 'to hug as our choicest treasure.' My friend has not this pleasure when he sits entranced in the stall that I have given up to him. James has not this pleasure when, knife in hand, he is cutting his name delightedly. It is I who have it, as I stand shivering in the passage. It is poor Bill who has it, with James's boots resting on his coat-collar.

Having thus far defined virtuous happiness

as a conception, we must now see how it is to be turned into a reality, how it is to be hoisted into the lofty niche designed for it, how it is to be made practically operative with those who we desire should seek it. As conceived of by the theist, it has three essential characteristics by which in his system it gains its hold on man— its inwardness, its importance, and (within limits) its absolute character. I have pointed these out in my former volume; and have declared that the theist could alone invest it with them. That the characteristics are essential both my positive critics declare loudly; but they declare also that they are quite independent of theism, and that the positive philosophy leaves them as marked as ever. Let us now proceed to examine again the two first of them, leaving the third to be dealt with later on, and see how the positive moralists try to make good their premisses.

First, then, as to the inwardness of virtue, as *virtue*—what do both parties confessedly mean by that? They mean that its excellence results in the will, not in the outward act. The virtue, *as a virtue*, with the special pleasure it brings with it, is complete when the will has triumphed; and it is regarded as good with reference to the person willing, not with reference to those others on whose behalf he has willed. Professor Clifford has declared this as loudly and as plainly as any one. The virtuous act, in the acting of it, has its distinctive character 'for ever,' he says, 'and no accidental failure of its good or evil fruits can possibly alter that.'[1] And the language of Miss Bevington herself shows that she quite agrees with him. When we call virtue inward, therefore, we mean that as a pleasure, as a possible end of action—in other words, *as virtue*—it is self-regarding. We mean that we are enabled to pay a certain debt to our neighbours, only because we make ourselves feel that we owe a certain debt to ourselves.

Next as to its special, its incalculable importance, our meaning is precisely similar. When, as an end of action, we declare that it is important a man should follow it, we mean that it is important to himself; important indeed by the way to others, but of special and incalculable importance to himself alone.

Let us now see how my positive critic defends herself, in continuing to ascribe to virtue these two special characteristics; and it will be plain

---

[1] Professor Clifford, *Ethics of Belief.*

at once that she, and her school in common with her, instead of defending their position, are in reality utterly and for ever abandoning it; and that they only seem to be not doing so because they retain certain marked words, though they have completely reversed the meaning of them. Thus, instead of vindicating for virtue in any way the inwardness we above have spoken of, she merely 'emphatically maintains' the here meaningless truism that virtue initiates in a certain 'set of . . . sensibilities in the individual'[1]—a thing which is not peculiar to virtue, but is at once common and essential to all free action whatsoever. Whilst as to its importance, she here not so much misses but inverts the meaning; for referring it not to the agent, but to the vast sum of events present and to come, external to him, she does indeed show this importance to be, in the case of each man, incalculable, but incalculable not because it is so large, but because it is so infinitesimally small.

It will be thus seen, and no one can more clearly though more unconsciously confess this than Miss Bevington, that virtue, as a personal end of action, is placed by the positivists in a

[1] Professor Clifford, *Ethics of Belief*.

completely new position; that everything supreme and special in its pleasures altogether evaporates, and that, were their account of it a true one, there would be no means of 'marrying it to existing human emotion.'[1]

It will be here again urged that the sympathetic appetite, or the motive power in virtue, even if not to be roused by argument in the individual man now, will be evolved to the needed strength amongst the individual men of the future. This theory, however—itself open to dispute—would, were it never so true, be nothing to the point here. The business of the moralist is not scientific prophecy, though he will doubtless call that to his aid. His business is with living men and women, and lies in educating their wavering and wayward wills; nay, unless he can manage to do this, the prophecy just alluded to must, he believes, be falsified. 'Positivism,' says my American critic, 'recognises that beyond a certain stage of development, changes in human destiny depend immediately on the combined knowledge, desire, and will of human beings.'[2] 'It is well aware, also, he

[1] *Nineteenth Century*, October 1879, p. 600.
[2] *The Value of Life*, p. 235.

adds, 'of the feebleness of the sympathetic instincts; and ... it proposes therefore to develop such sentiments by every practicable means.'[1] This development produces, when accomplished, virtue; and virtue, to make plainness doubly plain, we will define yet once more. It is, says Miss Bevington, 'a special meeting of two characteristics,' and these two characteristics are 'use and difficulty.'[2] It is, therefore, not only the intensification in the individual of the sympathetic appetite, but it is such an intensification when secured with a struggle by the will.

I repeat again, then, that to produce this struggle, still more to secure the final success of it, is a thing that the positive theory makes a logical impossibility. What that system professes to do, is, when stated nakedly, neither more nor less than this. Starting with unalloyed happiness—with a balance of pure gratification, as not merely the only right, but the only possible end of action, it professes to show that, as reaching us directly, this happiness is a thing to be despised and renounced by all of us; and

[1] *The Value of Life*, p. 205.
[2] *Nineteenth Century*, October 1879, p. 592.

that whilst despised as the subject of our own enjoyment, we are to fall down and adore it as an object of contemplation. But to show this is plainly a quite impossible feat. If the delight of James is in itself despicable, this delight does not become noble in Bill's case because it reaches him at second hand, and because personally he has foregone all share in it. If it is good in itself at all, it must be best at first hand. If it is great at all, it must be greater when there is no pain to detract from it. The positive system can indeed prove one thing with regard to virtue; but this is the exact opposite of what it wants to prove. It can prove that we should each of us be glad if the rest of the world was virtuous; but that we should each of us avoid to the utmost being virtuous ourselves. Let me consult Miss Bevington, and see if she does not agree with me. 'Virtue, as *virtue*,' she says, 'will never cease to be admirable, and for this reason. Man will always accord a very special kind of admiration to such conduct in another as forwards his own interest at that other's cost. . . . When, moreover, he receives the benefit of such struggle, without himself encountering its difficulty—in other words, receives his own good fortune as the result of his neighbour's struggle—not the death, burial, and oblivion of a thousand creeds will avail to hinder the *instinctively special* force of his admiration.'[1] In other words, our liking for virtue lies in this, that its presence in another saves us from the needing it in ourselves.

Now I am aware that the above account of the matter will seem at first sight to be nothing more than a parody. And that it is essentially absurd is without doubt true. But its absurdity does not prove that it is not a true analysis of the positive theory; but that the positive theory is not a true analysis of facts. That virtue, as a fact, may be in many cases possible without any assent to theism, or any conscious thought of it, is plain enough, and is denied by nobody. But this is just what the theist would expect; and, as we shall see presently, he can perfectly well account for it.

We must first note, however, that though such instances of virtue *might* be adduced in numbers by the positive writers, those which they do adduce generally are not true instances at all. They consist almost always in abstentions

[1] *Nineteenth Century*, October 1879, p. 591.

from three crimes or vices, murder, theft, and drunkenness. But such abstentions, though containing in them, as virtue does, a personal desire overbalanced by a desire not personal, for all this are yet not virtues. They lack, at least in most cases, the essential element, struggle. They are useful, but they are not difficult. A selfish nephew, desiring the death of a rich uncle, is not praised as virtuous because he does not kill him; nor, supposing he forbears to do so, although he could do so safely, do we conceive him to experience any virtuous rapture. Or let us take an instance that is yet more suggestive —one connected not with murder, but with what is next door to it—vindictive cruelty. A man in a rage with his wife yields to his passion, and begins to kick her wildly. This at first gives him unmixed gratification; but he finds in a few seconds that he is more annoyed by the scratches she inflicts on him than he is gratified by the kicks that he inflicts on her. He therefore at once checks his passion; and though it often again disturbs him, he never again yields to it. It is yet plainer here, that, in spite of his self-restraint, the man in question is not virtuous. And we have in this case a type of a large number of actions, which, though they all of them resemble virtues, yet could some of them never have been such, and have, some of them, in the course of progress long ceased to be so.

We are here brought to the question of virtue and evolution; and we are now in a position to appreciate two important facts about it. The first of these is that when virtuous conduct comes, through evolution, to be spontaneous conduct, it loses altogether its special character *as virtue*; and so, as far as such virtue is concerned with it, 'our choicest treasure' vanishes. The second point is that such evolution has brought us but a certain way; and, without conscious endeavour on our part, it cannot, as my American critic admits, take us further. We are standing now, as it were, on the stepping-stones of a dead savagery, and are asking both how and why we should painfully climb higher; at all events, we are only capable of virtue in so far as we are in this position.

And in this position it is that positivism fails to help us. To this *how*? and *why*? it can give no coherent answer. The only answer it can give has a radical flaw in it—a flaw, indeed, which its exponents at times perceive, but which, as we shall see presently, they utterly fail to remedy. What we want, as virtuous agents, to have scientifically made plain to us, is that certain pleasures that lie for us on the far side of pain are greater for us beyond comparison than those that lie on the near side. The superior amount of their pleasurableness is an 'inexpugnable element,' as Mr. Spencer says, 'in our conception of them.'

Now the pleasures in question are, as we have seen, vicarious; they are, so to speak, not self-luminous. What we require then in a satisfactory answer must be one of two things. One of these might be a proof that those pleasures which *are* self-luminous, that is, which are secured by us for others, so far exceed any that could be self-luminous for ourselves, that the mere reflection of the former will outshine the sunlight of the latter. But this, we see at once, is an impossibility. No such pleasures exist. Nor, even if they did, would their existence meet the needs of the case; for though they might, no doubt, excite virtue in a minority, yet from the very terms of the proposition, they could do so in a minority only. Those who enjoyed them directly would not be virtuous at all; whilst virtuous pleasure, so far from being the highest, would be nothing but a poor substitute, good for those only who could not get the original.

What we require to have proved, then, must be plainly something different. I must be shown, not that the moonlight that is reflected on me from my friend's pleasure, is brighter than any candle-light I could get from my own; not that it is brighter than my candle, but that it is brighter than what seems to be its own sun. Such is the nature of the phenomenon that we really have to account for. We get more out of the sack than we, as yet, seem to have put into it. And here at last we are getting near the secret. We here see that, as yet, we have not the whole matter before us, but that there must be some new element that remains to be taken account of. When Bill, in lifting James on his shoulders, is happier than James thus lifted, his greater happiness must have some source beyond its seeming one. Its only seeming source is the delight of James; but that delight is despicable and vulgar, and Bill is vulgar also, in so far as he thinks it delightful. But Bill's balance of pleasure which his self-denial brings with it, is of a character very different. On this the moralist will bestow all his best praise; and it is typical, for the positive moralist, of the pleasures of all virtue. And what has happened in producing it? A few pains and pleasures, all objectively trivial and unworthy of a refined man's notice, have been arranged together in a certain way by a *will*. And the result is that, as a modern poet has said of music,

Out of three sounds are framed, not a fourth sound, but a star.

Whence then—from what alien source, does this star-like pleasure come—this 'choicest treasure,' this 'blessedness,' which, as Mr. Spencer takes several pages to tell us, can be only some form of personal, of subjective gratification?[1] It is clear that it cannot derive its value from those enjoyments which the virtue, that alone secures it to us, shuffles from hand to hand. It must derive it from something else that can yield far greater pleasure than these; something that, through all our thoughts for others, we must each 'covet earnestly' for

[1] Vide *Data of Ethics*, pp. 41-44.

ourselves, and in which, through all denials of self, we are each to the utmost to indulge self.

The positivists admit, though they continually lose sight of the fact, that such a something is essential; and they declare, with much pomp of language, that their system supplies us with it. According to their account of it, it is this. It is an intense, a passionate, an adoring joy at the fact of the human race existing: or, to put it accurately, and in Mr. Spencer's language, at the fact of its presupposed existence having a 'balance of pleasures over pains' as a 'necessary concomitant.' This balance is presented to us by the positive system, as, for us, the one august and precious thing in the universe; as a vast treasury of the highest possible rapture, in the whole of which we may every one of us share, if we only contribute faithfully each our private mite to it. On this conception the positivists have bestowed the greatest pains. They have used every means at their disposal to make it splendid and alluring, and it seems, in many cases, to be actually doing the work it is designed to do. They seem actually to have aroused by it an emotion that can be 'married' to their 'theory of virtue,' and 'so sway the motives that underlie conduct.' This last fact we may admit readily; and it is not unnaturally conceived by many to be a conclusive and practical proof of the validity of the positive system. Such, however, is very far from being the case. In the first place, as we shall see by-and-by, the final object of emotion we have just been speaking of, though impressive enough under the limelight of the imagination, is disenchanted instantly by a touch of logical daylight. Whilst as to its reality being proved by its apparent efficacy, we will first proceed to see how the theist replies to that.

When the positivist points out to him the emotion in question as not existing only, but existing efficaciously, the theist replies that the emotion is doubtless there, but that its analysis is very different from what the other thinks it is. It is, says the theist, no mere delight in the fact of the human race existing, though under one of its aspects it may coincide with that. Primarily, he says, it is a delight in the will of God, and a conformity with it, more or less impassioned. Whatever else the individual takes it for, it really is this. Man is, on this theory, the child of God, and part of the child's nature is an innate love for his father, and an innate longing to please him, though these very often may not rightly understand themselves. The theist goes on to say that, unless they do understand themselves, they will not indeed lie dormant, still less be extinguished; but that their action will be uncertain and wayward, and will never give their possessor either true peace or guidance. Thus what they are always craving for, always goading him to seek for them, is a logical account of what they really mean and aim at. And what the theist maintains is, that his system can alone give them this; not that it is alone in, to some degree, touching them; still less, that it is alone in finding them at hand to be touched.[1]

Let us now see what the theistic system is; remembering, as we do so, that the propositions

[1] Miss Bevington and others completely misrepresent the matter, when they speak of the theist as maintaining that religion, or belief in God, has created conscience or virtue. What the theist maintains is that God, not the belief in God, has created them; and that the belief in God has developed them. When the relations between religion and virtue are spoken of, the others fail to distinguish the simple and obvious difference between the logical connection and the historical; and to see that though historically virtue may be prior to religion, religion logically is prior to virtue.

we shall find it to consist of are not to be here discussed as true statements of facts, but as true translations of a belief in facts that is already latent in us, under the form of feeling. The feeling in question is that of the supreme value of virtue, in other words, the supremacy of the pleasure it is attended by. Now, as the theist and the positivist both here agree about much, we will start with their points of agreement, and we shall so the better signalise the point where they part company. The theist, then, agrees with the positivist in accepting as virtues all those acts which the latter defines as such ; and he agrees that they all tend, as Miss Bevington says they do, ' to the slow amelioration of man's condition upon earth,'[1] or, as she explains herself more distinctly, 'to the securing him a maximum of comfort and a minimum of friction,' and this, too, for the largest number of generations possible. Here the positivist stops, and the theist goes on alone. The former says that the virtuous appetite has now met with its proper and sufficient object in such vague happiness as is called comfort for an indefinite number of human beings. The theist altogether

[1] *Nineteenth Century,* December 1879, p. 1012.

denies this. The virtuous appetite, he says, is not satisfied that these human beings should be happy. This is an object that not only does not satisfy the appetite, but barely even excites it. It is not enough, he says, that these human beings should be happy, but that their happiness should be of one special kind. And for such special happiness he has a special name, and that name is holiness. Granted that man as man is capable of this, it at once becomes his duty to labour for man's existence; and a new meaning shoots for him into that result of virtue which Miss Bevington can describe only as its 'lifeward tendency.'

What, then, is holiness, that such should be the result of our recognition of it? In the answer to this question we have all theism in embryo. Holiness is a form of happiness so apart, and by itself, that it can be described, to those who have not felt it, no more than any simple taste can. To those who do not feel it the theist is dumb; for morally such men are for the theist, deaf. But for those who do feel it or can remember once to have felt it, what the theist says is sufficiently plain and moving. They will know what he means, however vague his language, when he tells them it is a feeling,

> Unde nil majus generatur ipso,
> Nec viget quidquam simile aut secundum;

and that life, except as a selfish and contemned pleasure, is of value only as being the condition of this. They will know what he means when he tells them further that this feeling unites in itself two qualities, which in all the positive virtues are of necessity in antagonism —selfishness and unselfishness; that there is here a perfect marriage and balance between the pair, and that neither of them is afore or after the other. They will know what he means when he tells them finally that the one cause and source of this feeling is the vision and the fruition of God; and that the saint when he exclaims, 'My Lord, I desire nothing but thee,' is exclaiming in the same breath, 'and that my brother may desire thee also.'

In this desire, says the theist, in this supreme desire, though it often does its work in secret and in ways past finding out, is the real motive for all those painful acts which the positivists praise as virtues because of their 'lifeward tendency,' meaning only by this that they conduce to general 'comfort.' The theist values life, and he values lifeward tendencies, not as subserving comfort, but as subserving holiness. That men should live and be holy, is, he believes, God's will; and to co-operate with that will in all ways is the essence of holiness. It is thus that the theory of lifeward actions is for him 'married to the emotions,' and 'so sways the motives that underlie conduct.'

But what, then, of those direct pleasures of life, which it is but fair to suppose that Miss Bevington includes in 'comfort?' What of the pleasures, the excitements, and, above all, the affections with which for most of us the entire daily landscape is occupied, and amongst which exclusively our active work lies? What account does the theist give of these, that is in harmony with common sense, and with the common estimate of them? The account he gives is complete; and it is the only account that can justify the manner in which they are regarded at present and in which the positivists declare they shall never cease to be regarded. All the pleasures, he says, and all the comforts in question, are arranged in a scale, ascending and descending according to their relation to the supreme pleasure of holiness. Some of them are incompatible with it, and from their very nature quench it. These are the fleshly lusts that war against the Spirit. Others, though not it, are yet imbued with a portion of it, some in a greater degree, some less; until into the thirst for knowledge and into chastened human affection, there seems to have been transubstituted the very thing itself.

But we must here note this. These pleasures, even the highest of them, though they must be granted to us as sacraments of holiness, are yet in themselves distinct from holiness. The good man may long to acquire knowledge; the good man may long to receive love. But he may be called upon, also, to forego both; and if he respond to this call of God willingly and with his whole heart, he will be not the less holy, but the holier. It is essential to the entire position that we remember this. For were this not the case, the system of the theist would be as faulty as the system of the positivist. Each system requires alike that we should, if asked to do so, surrender all pleasures but one. But the theistic system alone can supply such a pleasure which, through all self-surrender, will still remain for ever with us.

This system, however, whilst denying any pleasures but this one to be necessary, yet admits others as good in a deep, though secondary, sense; not despising those even which, as related to holiness, seem at first to be most indifferent. I speak of those very pleasures which alone Miss Bevington and her school dwell upon—those pleasures or comforts, on the general distribution of which the continuance of the human race, in the long run, depends; and with which alone, on their theory, virtue has to deal. The pursuit of holiness does not force us aside from these; for these, so far as they are 'lifeward in their tendency,' are all of them in accordance with the will of God. Nor does the pursuit of holiness fail to give a meaning to the allaying at our own cost of the slightest pain in another; or to giving another, at our own cost, the slighest innocent pleasure. The theist agrees with the positivist that such actions are virtues, and that they bring a pleasure with them that far outweighs their pain. But the virtuous pleasure that lures us to such self-denial, comes not from the pleasure foregone, which *ex hypothesi* is indifferent, but from the oblation, conscious or unconscious, of self-denial, to God. If its after consequences have been really lifeward, well and good. We shall so have been forwarding his will. But even should they fail entirely our act is not in vain. It is good in itself, in its own nature. In Professor Clifford's words, 'no accidental failure of its fruits can possibly alter that.' It is good in its effect on ourselves as a surrender of ourselves to God. It is the giving Him the best that the moment has enabled us to give Him; it is what He values most, the conforming of our *will* to His. And such an act in one single man is an exemplar of what should be the acts of all men—an exemplar, not because its results as a fact are valuable, but because with all earnestness they have been meant to be so. For the positivist the only measure of virtue is the objective success of it; or, as Miss Bevington puts it, its active realised 'use.' But the theist, should God deny all such use to it, can rest in faith; and should it prove useful he will rest in thankfulness. Paul has planted, Apollos watered; but it is God that has given the increase.

Here we see what the theist means when he

says that virtue is inward; here we see what he means when he says it is all-important. And now we can see what he means when he says its character is absolute. He does not mean the poor truism of the positivist which no one contradicts or ever dreamed of contradicting, that the conduct conducing to certain social advantages cannot be altered by the changing caprice of each of us. He means that amongst the pleasures of which these advantages are, by the other's confession, the negative conditions only, there is one pleasure supreme over all the others, and to whose throne the others are valuable only as steps. We now see what and whence is that pure and perfect passion which, when once sure of its end, gives a meaning to all virtue.

And in seeing this, we must also have seen more than this. We must have seen that whilst the theist admits, as virtues, all the acts that positivists define as such, he includes a further set that the positivist cannot include. He includes not only the subjugation of our own pleasures as warring against others' happiness; but the subjugation of our own lower pleasures, as warring against our own holiness. And *logically*, in our conception of virtue, it is this last-named part of it that is the first. My desire for holiness must first make my life precious to me, before I can attach much preciousness to the lives of other people. Thus the meaning of the word virtue is at once immeasurably widened; and its present popular use is explained naturally. I will but quote one instance, and that shall be the commonest and the most significant—the popular identification of virtue with sexual continence. What is implied here is, not that chastity is a virtue because externally it is of social use to others, but because internally it prepares self for God; because it is a part of the payment of that same debt to Him, of which subserving the welfare of others is another part, and a part logically subordinate.

Here is the explanation of that ambiguity in my language, which I said just now I would correct—my use at times, in my former volume, of the words virtue and morality as synonymous with the highest happiness, and with the final end of life. I should, to have been entirely accurate, have named that end not virtue but holiness; and, for the sake of entire clearness, let me do so now. Let me re-state my former proposition, with its meaning unchanged, but only with its terms amended. Let me say that what positivism subtracts from life, utterly and for ever, is primarily not virtue as virtue, but holiness as holiness; to which I add, in what is here only a parenthesis, that, in destroying the latter, it also destroys the former; leaving us indeed, as its objects, many reasons to wish for it; but as agents, no motive that can make us practise even a part of it.

Holiness then, let me remind Miss Bevington and all those who agree with her, is the real name of the thing that their system takes away from them. And indeed, though they do not use the word in question, they make no secret that there is some such loss. But what they fail to see is the extent and the result of it. Miss Bevington in her last Essay informs us that we have lost nothing but 'a moral sofa,' and 'our spiritual cakes and ale.' This is her simile for the sense of trust in God.[1] But I

---

[1] 'Our "unbelievers" know what they lose in losing religion. They lose their moral sofas, their spiritual "cakes and ale;" but the solid ground remains for spiritual exercise, and the bread and meat of success and survival will continue to reward that exercise wherever faithfully performed.'

can tell her that the loss she speaks of is indeed a loss, not only of 'spiritual cakes and ale,' but of necessary food and drink—of food and drink without which the soul dies of starvation; producing those results, during its lingering, painful death, which my critic herself describes as 'thoroughly dismal and sickening.'

If she and her school deny this, out of their own mouth I can judge them; and for such witness I need go no further than the words of my present critic herself. Throughout the whole of her two essays, what she is really appealing to, is no sense on our part that virtue produces comfort, which, besides its difficulty, is the only charactistic she gives it; but a sense that it is valuable as connected with that hierarchy of ascending pleasures, which are ranged in due gradation about the throne of holiness. Thus 'greedy seizure on handy pleasure' she thinks need be named merely to be at once condemned by us; and she puts the 'bliss of the moment' in contrast with 'the strength of the morrow:'[1] although bliss and pleasure are, she affirms, the only things to live for; although strength

---

[1] *Nineteenth Century*, December 1879, p. 1006.

has no value except as a means of bliss; and although the value of bliss, she says, depends on itself, and not on the 'hours or the years' for which it is or will be present. Again, there are two classes, she says, for whom we must labour; one is 'sufferers,' and the other is '*sinners*.'[1] Sexual passion she describes as in itself a 'reeking miasm;'[2] and yet more significantly she says she has 'not the least *fear*'[3] that its admitted pleasures will ever receive the approval of positivism. Why, let me ask her, should she use the word 'fear'? Surely on her own grounds she should have said 'hope' instead. The pleasures she alludes to are for many men very keen pleasures. Could they then only be found not injurious to the general 'comfort,' the world would, on her own grounds, be so much the richer for enjoying them. My critic is plainly quite sincere in her feelings; but they belong to the creed she denies, not to the creed she is defending. She really hates vice because it wars against the spirit of holiness; not because it wars in any way against the spirit of comfort. But she makes this plainer yet in

[1] *Nineteenth Century*, December 1879. [2] *Ibid.*
[3] *Ibid.* October 1879, p. 591.

another place. Fortunately, as an illustration of the present condition of the positivists, she has published a small volume of verse, in which the restless movements—I might almost say the antics—of theism are pathetically visible under the donkey's skin of positivism. The following lines are from the most prominent and the most powerful of the poems :—

> But now—what says philosophy of Self?
> What thinks her follower of the man he is?
> Can he, in presence of the symphony
> That rolls around him, played by viewless cause,
> On suns for instruments, with life for key. . . .
> Can he revert to his small destiny
> As worth a moment's stopping of his ears,
> While that sweet thundering of the huge 'Not Self
> Challenges him to listen while he may?'[1]

Now what do these lines mean as explained by the professed theories of their writer? The 'huge Not Self' seems here to mean what she calls in another place 'nature's large impersonal workings ;' and in these she says 'we do like to think there is an end that we may make our special personal *own*.'[2] But 'the unbelieving moralist,' she goes on immediately, 'must resign

---

[1] *Key Notes*, by L. S. Bevington, 1879, p. 16.
[2] *Nineteenth Century*, October 1879, p. 601.

the luxury of such a belief.' If this be the case, in what possible sense can the 'huge Not Self' be said to 'thunder' at all, still more, to 'thunder sweetly'? In Wordsworth's ears it is quite true it did: for him it was a shell that murmured with the voice of God. But Miss Bevington's case is altogether different. Perhaps, however, the 'huge Not Self' means what she elsewhere calls 'many-millioned humanity.' But in that case her meaning is no more satisfactory. If every self is paltry, so are all selves put together. If the talking of one man is senseless babble, the united babbling of a million men may indeed 'out-thunder' it; but the 'thundering' will be neither 'sweet' nor sensible. Let us take a case of a like confusion in her prose, to which the mention of 'Humanity' at once conducts us. 'The evolutionist,' she tells us, 'feels (through virtue) the glow of a calm blessedness in contemplating a mass of human beings'—and why? Because 'his own smallest achievement in self-education and self-elevation cannot but affect them beneficially. There is no small and great for him, since all is effectual.'[1] In this language we have a still more evident survival

[1] *Nineteenth Century*, December 1879, p. 1008.

of theism, for in the mouth of the theist it has a distinct meaning ; in the mouth of the positivist none. Let the will be good, and for the theist there is indeed no small and great objectively. But for the positivist the case is otherwise. The 'mass of human beings' cannot thus take the will for the deed ; and our virtues are great and small in exact proportion to results they accomplish severally. For the positivists to say that there is no small or great in them is as if a railway company were to say to the public, 'Pay us with two pence or two pounds for your tickets ; there is neither much nor little with us for all is effectual.'

What Miss Bevington has here had in her mind is what Christ said of the widow's mite ; but in attempting to transplant this from His system to hers she shows not the difference only, but the antagonism of the two. The 'mass of human beings,' as an object of work and ardour, can never supply the place of God, nor does it go even the smallest way towards doing so. Every effort made by the positivists to invest it with the divine glory and to raise it to the divine eminence fails. They attempt to perform the feat in many ways, but each effort ends in its own discomfiture; and the logic they invoke to aid them by-and-by turns round and confounds them. We are to adore humanity, they say, as a vast corporate Pleasure, and our emotions are to make us serve it by our each doing our all to add to it. But the coin, they proceed to tell us, in which our several shares are to be paid is self-denial, and toil, and difficulty. And thus the idol they hoped to show us as a gigantic pleasure confronts them as nothing but a sum-total of pains. Then, again, if swerving from this conclusion, they seek to fix the mind on life's direct and personal pleasures, they find that they are already pledged in each case to speak of these as contemptible; and their system thus demands of them the new paradox that the sum of countless negative quantities is a vast positive total. Whilst, finally, if they appeal to the feeling they find existing for virtue, and trust to rouse a response, when they call it 'our choicest treasure,' they are confronted by their system with this blighting doctrine, that the one final end which it bids us hope for is that virtue shall work itself out of, not into, the great human entity. That, unconsciously, they feel all this themselves is apparent whenever they forget their logic, and trust themselves for a moment to utter their own emotions; never more so than when they fly off at a tangent, and appeal to 'stars' and 'suns,' and 'æons,' and all the fine things in the extra-human universe.

That the emotion that prompts such language is genuine, none need doubt; nor will the theist deny to it all fitting respect. But the more reverend he considers the emotion of the positivists, the more completely ludicrous does he consider their own analysis of it. What he sees in it is a survival of the religion they deny; not the firstfruits of the irreligion they profess. Positivism, as preached in France, has been called by Professor Huxley 'Catholicism minus Christianity.' As preached in England and America, it may be called similarly 'Methodism minus Christianity.' That Methodism contains in it the sense of holiness, the sense of sin, and the longing to co-operate with God's will—we all of us know this. But this is not positivism.

What is positivism? Is the theory true or false that, independent of our own wills, or in defiance of them, our race is tending steadily to get rid of its own discomforts? And the positivists present this race to us as one single individual, whose vast career it imagines will inflame and move us. But this 'huge Not Self,' presented to the lover of virtue, so far from being better than the small 'selves' that compose it, must really seem but the type of what is worst and lowest in them. Humanity, regarded as a single being, is a being without any aspirations that are not selfish, and without any duties at all. It has been bestial at its infancy, savage in its youth, unutterably impure in its manhood; and as a worthy crown of a worthy life, it is to simper at last through an unrepentant dotage into a hopeless and unremembered grave.

I have alluded in this essay to Miss Bevington's remarks on myself, only in so far as they seem convenient examples of the reasonings of the school she is representing. But if I may say at parting a single word to herself, I would remind her that all that her new teachers can tell her about virtue has been told the world long ago by Christianity. They have not contributed a single new truth to it; though doubtless to prove its truth they may have subpœnaed new witnesses. All that they have done new is not to add to the Christian teaching, but to subtract from it; and to subtract from it the one part that alone gave the whole vitality.

>Oh the little more, and how much it is!
> And the little less, and what worlds away!
>How a sound shall quicken content to bliss,
> Or a touch suspend the blood's best play—
>And life be a proof of this!

G.

A LIST OF NEW WORKS
Preparing for Autumn Publication.

By the CROWN PRINCE OF AUSTRIA.
Travels in the East. Including a Visit to the Holy Land, Egypt, the Ionian Islands, &c. By His Imperial and Royal Highness the CROWN PRINCE RUDOLPH. In royal 8vo. with numerous Illustrations.

By EDMUND YATES.
Memoirs of a Man of the World; or, Fifty Years of London Life. By EDMUND YATES. In 2 vols. demy 8vo. with portraits and vignettes.

Edited by LORD BRABOURNE.
Letters of Jane Austen to her Relations, 1796-1815. Hitherto Unpublished. Edited, with Introduction and Notes, by the Right Hon. LORD BRABOURNE. In 2 vols. large crown 8vo. with frontispieces.

By MR. SERJEANT BALLANTINE.
From the Old World to the New. Being some Experiences of a Recent Visit to America, including a Trip to the Mormon Country. By Mr. SERJEANT BALLANTINE, Author of 'Some Experiences of a Barrister.' In demy 8vo. with portrait.

By MRS. SPEEDY.
My Wanderings in the Soudan. By Mrs. T. C. S. SPEEDY. In 2 vols. crown 8vo. with numerous Illustrations.

By J. J. HISSEY.
An Old-Fashioned Journey through England and Wales. By JAMES JOHN HISSEY. In demy 8vo. With frontispiece.

By H. W. LUCY.
East by West. A Record of Travel round the World. By HENRY W. LUCY, Author of 'Gideon Fleyce,' &c. In 2 vols. cr. 8vo.

By LADY WILDE.
Driftwood from Scandinavia. By FRANCESCA LADY WILDE. In 1 volume, large crown 8vo.

By C. PHILLIPPS-WOLLEY.
The Trottings of a 'Tender Foot' in Spitzbergen and British Columbia. By CLIVE PHILLIPPS-WOLLEY, F.R.G.S., Author of 'Sport in the Crimea and Caucasus.' In 1 vol. crown 8vo.

By ROBERT BUCHANAN.
Reminiscences of a Literary Career: An Autobiography. By ROBERT BUCHANAN. In 2 vols. crown 8vo. with portrait. [December 31.

By LADY FULLERTON.
Ellen Middleton. By LADY GEORGIANA FULLERTON, Author of 'Too Strange not to be True,' &c. A new edition in 1 vol. crown 8vo. 6s.

By M. DE BOURRIENNE.
Memoirs of Napoleon Bonaparte. By LOUIS ANTOINE FAUVELET DE BOURRIENNE, his Private Secretary. Edited, with Preface and Notes, by Colonel R. W. PHIPPS, late Royal Artillery. In 3 vols. demy 8vo. with Map and the following Illustrations, except one, on steel:

VOL. I.	VOL. II.	VOL. III.
Napoleon I. (a).	Josephine (a).	Maria Louise (a).
Pichegru.	Lannes.	King of Rome.
Moreau.	Macdonald.	Bessieres.
Desaix.	Cuirassiers at Eylau.	Duroc.
Kleber.	Murat.	Caulaincourt.
Duc d'Enghien.	Napoleon I. (b).	MariaLouise(b),
Letitia Ramolino.	Josephine (b)	Prince Eugene.
Talleyrand.	Davoust.	Napoleon I. (c).
Hortense.	Lasalle.	The Abdication
Junot.	Suchet.	Wellington.
Ney (a).	GouvionSt.Cyr.	Blucher.
Massena.	Soult.	Ney (b)

By STANLEY HARRIS.
Reminiscences of the Road. By STANLEY HARRIS, Author of 'Old Coaching Days.' With 16 Illustrations on stone by John Sturgess. In demy 8vo.

By Mrs. MOSS KING.
Diary of a Civilian's Wife in India. By Mrs. MOSS KING. In 2 vols. crown 8vo. with numerous Illustrations from drawings by the Author.

By A. J. WEISE.
A History of the Discoveries of America down to the Year 1525. By ARTHUR JAMES WEISE, M.A. In 1 vol. demy 8vo. with numerous Maps reproduced in facsimile from the originals.

By W. H. MALLOCK.
Literary Essays. By WILLIAM HURRELL MALLOCK, Author of 'Is Life worth Living?' &c. In 1 vol. crown 8vo.

ANONYMOUS.
Letters from Hell. Newly translated from the German. With an Introduction by Dr. GEORGE MACDONALD. In 1 vol. crown 8vo. 6s.

By DEAN HOOK.
The Lives of the Archbishops of Canterbury. By WALTER FARQUHAR HOOK, D.D., late Dean of Chichester. Reissues of Volumes VIII. and XII. in demy 8vo.

By LADY JACKSON.
The Court of France in the Sixteenth Century in the Reigns of Francis I. and Henry II. By CATHERINE CHARLOTTE LADY JACKSON, Author of 'Old Paris,' 'The Old Régime,' &c. In 2 vols. large crown 8vo. with portraits. [December 31.

By HECTOR MALOT.
No Relations. By HECTOR MALOT. A new edition, with numerous Illustrations, in 1 vol. crown 8vo. in red cloth, 6s.

RICHARD BENTLEY & SON, NEW BURLINGTON STREET,
Publishers in Ordinary to Her Majesty the Queen.

A NEW LIBRARY EDITION OF
MISS FERRIER'S NOVELS.
(THE EDINBURGH EDITION.)

In Six Volumes small crown 8vo.

The Set 30s. (originally published at 21s.), or separately as under:—

MARRIAGE	**2 Vols. 10s.**
THE INHERITANCE . . .	**2 Vols. 10s.**
DESTINY	**2 Vols. 10s.**

This Edition is printed from the Original Edition as annotated by the Author, of whom a short Memoir is prefixed in 'Marriage.'

'Edgeworth, Ferrier, Austen, have all given portraits of real society far superior to anything man, vain man, has produced of the like nature.'
—SIR WALTER SCOTT.

'Miss Ferrier's novels are all thick set with specimens of sagacity, happy traits of nature, flashes of genuine satire, easy humour, sterling good sense, and above all—God only knows where she picked it up—mature and perfect knowledge of the world.'—NOCTES AMBROSIANÆ.

'I retire from the field, conscious there remains behind not only a large harvest, but labourers capable of gathering it in. More than one writer has of late displayed talents of this description, and if the present author, himself a phantom, may be permitted to distinguish a brother, or perhaps a sister shadow, he would mention in particular the author of the very lively work entitled "Marriage."'—SIR WALTER SCOTT.

'I assure you I think it ("Marriage") without exception the cleverest thing that ever was written, and in wit far surpassing Fielding.'
—LADY CHARLOTTE BURY.

'On Wednesday I dined in company with Sir Walter Scott, and he spoke of the work ("The Inheritance") in the very highest terms. I do not always set the highest value on the baronet's favourable opinion of a book, because he has so much kindness of feeling towards every one, but in this case he spoke so much *con amore*, and entered so completely, and at such length to me, into the spirit of the book and of the characters, that showed me at once the impression it had made upon him. Every one I have met who has seen the book gives the same praise of it.'—JOHN BLACKWOOD.

'On the day of the dissolution of Parliament, and in the critical hours between twelve and three, I was employed in reading part of the second volume of "Destiny." My mind was so completely occupied on your colony in Argyleshire, that I did not throw away a thought on kings or parliaments, and was not moved by the general curiosity to stir abroad until I had finished your volume. It would have been nothing if you had so agitated a youth of genius and susceptibility, prone to literary enthusiasm, but such a victory over an old hack is perhaps worthy of your notice.'
—MACKINTOSH (to Miss Ferrier).

To be obtained of all Booksellers.

RICHARD BENTLEY & SON, NEW BURLINGTON STREET,
Publishers in Ordinary to Her Majesty the Queen.

www.ingramcontent.com/pod-product-compliance
Lightning Source LLC
Chambersburg PA
CBHW032045220426
43664CB00008B/866